La Cocina Italiana

Four Seasons of Italian Cooking

La Cucina Italiana

Four Seasons of Italian Cooking

ARMANDO PERCUOCO • DAVID DALE

RAINCOAST BOOKS

Vancouver

Contents

List of Recipes   5

Introduction   8

Glossary   10

General Recipes   12

Spring   14

Summer   44

Autumn   82

Winter   120

Index   154

Acknowledgements   158

General Recipes

Neapolitan Sauce 12
Meat Stock 12
Basic Sponge 13
Basic Polenta 13
Whipped Mascarpone 13
Semifreddo 13

∼

Spring Menu One

Finocchiara 17
Fennel and Artichoke Salad

Linguine with Pesto Sauce 17

Perch Puccini 18

Torta di Riso 19
Rice Cakes

∼

Spring Menu Two

Zuppa di Verdure 23
Vegetable Soup

Insalata Fantasia 24
Roast Pork and Mushroom Salad

Pollo al Rosmarino 24
Rosemary Chicken

Fettuccine con Pomodoro 25
Strawberry "Pasta"

∼

Spring Menu Three

Gamberi con Fagioli 29
Prawns with Beans

Cotolette alla Pompeano 30
Pork with Red Cabbage

Frutta Gratinata 31
Baked Fruit

∼

Spring Menu Four

Seafood Lasagna 35

Agnello Primavera 36
Roast Lamb with Sweet Potato Puree

Cassata Siciliana 37

∼

Spring Menu Five

Bruschetta 41

Spaghetti with Mussels and Clams 41

Involtini 42
Veal Rolls with Emmenthal and Cabbage

Poached Peaches with Amaretti Biscuits 43

∼

Summer Menu One

Antipasto of Stuffed Eggplant & Capsicums
with Anchovy Dressing 47-48

Calamari with Olive Paste 49

Beef with Salsa Verde 50

Semifreddo with Prunes 51

∼

Summer Menu Two

Spaghetti Tricolore 55
Spaghetti with Tomatoes and Arugola

Quaglie del Cardinale 56
Quails with Cherries

Pesche nel Tempio 57
"Temples" with Peach Puree

∼

Summer Menu Three

Fichi Biondi 61
Figs with Gorgonzola Sauce

Orata d'Estate 62
Snapper with Mint

Fruit "Pizza" 63

∾

Summer Menu Four

Carpaccio Salmonato 67

Angel Hair Pasta with Sage 67

Zuppa di Pesce 68
Fish Soup

Cherry Cake 69

∾

Summer Menu Five

Rollata di Peperoni 73
Rolled Capsicum with Goat's Cheese

Roast Salmon with Asparagus 74

Torta di Fichi 75
Fig and Mascarpone Cake

∾

Summer Menu Six
A PICNIC LUNCH

Frittata di Maccheroni &
Marinated Zucchini & Insalata Caprese 79-80
*Pasta and Egg Pie & Marinated Zucchini
& Tomato and Mozzarella Salad*

Pane Rustico 80
Cheese Bread

Pollo alla Diavola 81
Peppered Chicken

Fresh Fruit & Parmesan Cheese 81

∾

Autumn Menu One

Orecchiette Pasta with Broccoli 85

Grilled Quails with Eggplant Puree 86

Dolce dell'Angelo 87
Sweet Pasta Pie

∾

Autumn Menu Two

Antipasto of Mushroom Frittata & Stuffed
Zucchini & Spicy Cauliflower 91-92

Truffled Eggs 93

Involtini di Salmone 94
Salmon Rolls

Torta di Mandorle 95
Almond Cake

∾

Autumn Menu Three

Penne with Saffron 99

Octopus Casserole 100

Frolla Napoli 101

∾

Autumn Menu Four

Torta di Polenta 105
Polenta, Pumpkin, and Spinach Cake

Pollo alla Marsala 106
Chicken Legs with Porcini Mushrooms and Marsala

Coppa d'Autunno 107
Fruit Sundae

∾

Autumn Menu Five

Linguine in Cartoccio 111
Seafood Pasta Parcel

Salsicce alla Toscana 112
Spicy Sausages and Beans

Insalata di Montagna 112
Radicchio Salad with Bacon and Goat's Cheese

Pere al Cioccolato 113
Baked Pears with Chocolate Sauce

∾

Autumn Menu Six

Pumpkin Risotto 117

Hot Beef Carpaccio with Polenta 118

Formaggi e Canditi Misti 119
Cheeses and Dried Fruits

∾

Winter Menu One

Zuppa con Polpette 123
Chicken Soup with Meat Balls

Farfalle con le Mandorle 123
Butterfly Pasta with Almond Sauce

Involtini di Spinaci 124
Veal Rolls with Spinach

Torta di Mele 125
Apple Cake

∾

Winter Menu Two

Ribollita 129
Tuscan Bread Soup

Bistecca alla Lombardia 130
Roast Beef with Pureed Beets and Pumpkin Gnocchi

Pere alla Vivaldi 131
Stuffed Pears

∾

Winter Menu Three

Arancini 135
Rice Balls with Peas and Mozzarella

Tonno alla Siciliana 136
Tuna with Sweet Chillies

Torta di Neve 137
Cherry "Soufflé"

∾

Winter Menu Four

Antipasto of Fave con Pancetta & Funghi in
Padella & Barbecued Eggplant 141-142
*Antipasto of Beans with Bacon & Mushrooms with
Chilli & Barbecued Eggplant*

Gnocchi Verdi 143
Spinach and Ricotta Dumplings

Osso Pieno 144
Veal Knuckle in Red Wine

Zabaglione 145

∾

Winter Menu Five

Pappardelle Pasta with Duck Sauce 149

Maiale d'Inverno 150
Rolled Pork

Fennel and Radicchio Salad 151

Tartufo di Cioccolato 152
Intense Chocolate Pudding

∾

Introduction

The news about Italian cooking is all good. First, it's easy. Second, it's tasty. Third, it's immensely diverse, reflecting the fact that Italy is really 20 different countries loosely linked into one nation. And fourth, it's healthy, without even trying to be.

The core ingredients of what is known these days as "the Mediterranean diet"—pasta, vegetables, olive oil, garlic, and seafood—seem to be ideal for reducing the risk of heart disease and other internal disorders. And Italians always eat seasonally, using foods that are fresh (ripened by nature rather than chemistry), and staying in harmony with the climate. With such virtuous elements at the centre of so many recipes, there's no reason for guilt about the occasional indulgence, and we've taken that liberty from time to time in this book.

Italians believe that pleasure is more important than work, and that philosophy is reflected in their approach to cooking. They love their food, but they don't want to spend hours fussing with it to achieve some pretentious artistic effect. They'd rather let the flavours of good ingredients speak for themselves. They're happy to leave other nations to disguise flavours with heavy spicing, or blend and mould ingredients so that the dish looks like an untouchable sculpture. Over the centuries, Italians have developed a catalogue of recipes that enables even the most nervous beginner to become a generous host.

As you experiment with the meals in this book you'll find that it's very hard to make a mistake. Some recipes are our renovations of traditional favourites, and some are new creations within the Italian way of doing things, but all are part of the most robust cooking style in the world. We've given precise quantities for the ingredients and precise instructions for combinations and cooking times, but you can treat them as a rough guide, and make variations according to your own taste—a little less chilli, a little more garlic, a different mix of herbs, an extra splash of liqueur, icecream instead of mascarpone, lemon instead of vinegar, and so on. Imagination tempered by common sense should allow the cook to have even more fun than the guests.

We hope that this book, like its inspiration, will be easy and diverse. We suggest you start your menu planning by reading the introductions—they contain a little historical and cultural background and a lot of advice on suitable accompaniments and ideas for serving and presentation. (Since colour is an important stimulant to appetite, our combinations are designed to satisfy your visual sense as well.)

We hope you won't be straitjacketed by the menus. They are designed to provide balanced meals, but after you've become familiar with them, you should feel free to mix and match—perhaps winter dishes won't always sit well with summer dishes, but there's every reason to try an antipasto from spring with a main course from summer and a dessert from autumn. Like all eating, this book should be an adventure.

Let's begin the journey by looking at a few fundamentals of Italian food and our approach to it...

THE CORE RECIPES

Certain ingredients recur frequently in Italian cooking and therefore in our menus, so we thought it best to describe them here. There is also a glossary in which you can look up any unfamiliar terms you come across in the book (see page 10), and recipes for some of the elements that appear in more than one menu (see page 12).

These basics include the mother of all sauces—tomatoes, oil, garlic, and basil—best known as Neapolitan sauce. It's good enough by itself to throw on pasta when you're in a hurry and seeking a light snack, and it adds a surge of Mediterranean sunshine to many a more elaborate dish. There's also an intense meat stock which we like to use as a dressing for some dishes (it even works with calamari), and as part of the

cooking process for others. And there's polenta, a kind of corn meal porridge beloved in the north of Italy. It can be served soft to soak up gamey sauces, or grilled and cut into crunchy squares as a side dish.

In the dessert area, we have the world's easiest icecream, a luscious mix of cream and eggs known to Italians as semifreddo. And there's our version of mascarpone, whipped up with egg whites, which can be a treat in itself with sweet biscuits, or a dressing for any fruity dessert.

PASTA—SHAPE MATTERS AND TIME MATTERS

The last time anybody did a census of the different shapes of pasta available in Italy, they stopped counting at 600: ribbons and wheels and strings and shells and sheets and bowties and flying saucers and so on. Although it might be said that all pastas are just manipulations of flour and water, Italians believe that particular shapes work better with particular sauces, because of the way the sauce adheres to the surface and the way air circulates in the mouth. So while you may not always be able to buy the exact pasta we nominate for a dish, we hope you'll try to come close: for example, fettuccine should be replaced by some other flat ribbon style that is not too wide, while angel hair should be replaced by the thinnest spaghetti you can find.

Italians also do not believe in cooking pasta until it's totally soft. They like it "al dente", offering a little resistance to the teeth. The cooking times we've suggested (for example, 7 minutes for spaghetti) will produce an al dente texture, so adjust these times if you have a different preference. But try our method first—al dente is a quickly acquired taste.

OLIVE OIL—VIRGINITY MATTERS

A lot of nonsense is talked about olive oil these days, but two facts are indisputable: as a cooking medium, it's far healthier than butter or other fats, and as a dressing for salads or soups, extra virgin olive oil tastes far better than ordinary oil. The term "extra virgin" means the oil is extracted simply by pressing the olives, and not by heating them or applying chemicals to them. The extra virgin oil is heavier (and more expensive) than the processed stuff, so we suggest you use the ordinary oil for cooking and keep the extra virgin for dressings and for drizzling over soup and vegetables.

GARLIC—HEAT MATTERS

Cooked garlic is a very different creature from raw garlic. We hardly ever use raw garlic in our recipes because it can overpower everything, yet we often use cooked garlic because it is sweet and pungent and brings out the best in many other savoury ingredients. Too much frying, however, can burn garlic and taint the dish with a bitter taste. So here's the hint: don't preheat the olive oil. Put it and the garlic together in a pan at room temperature and then place the pan on just above medium heat. If your stove is electric, let the hotplate warm up for a couple of minutes before placing the pan on it. If the garlic is crushed or minced, fry it for about 30 seconds. If it is in chunks or cloves, fry it for a minute. When it starts to look golden (not brown) the magical transformation has taken place.

And so begin your year of pursuing happiness in the Italian way. Buon viaggio and buon appetito.

Glossary

AMARETTI

Small, hard, almond-flavoured biscuits, useful for crumbling as dessert toppings.

AMARETTO

Sweet, almond-flavoured high-alcohol liqueur.

ANGEL HAIR PASTA (CAPELLI D'ANGELO)

The thinnest noodles in existence.

ARBORIO RICE

The fat, fluffy form of rice favoured by Italians.

ARUGOLA (ALSO KNOWN AS RUCOLA AND ROCKET)

Dark green, peppery-tasting leaves excellent in salads and as accompaniments to rich main courses.

BALSAMIC VINEGAR

A mellow vinegar, coming from what is called a "vinegar mother", which has been aged in wood.

BEL PAESE

A semi-soft, mild cheese from the north of Italy.

BOCCONCINI

Golf-ball size spheres of mozzarella cheese (often made with buffalo milk in Italy).

BORLOTTI BEANS

Medium-sized red or speckled beans which should be soaked overnight before cooking.

BROAD BEANS

Nutritious, strong-flavoured beans, sometimes green, sometimes light brown. The dried type are best soaked for 24 hours before cooking.

CANDIED FRUIT (CANDITI)

Small pieces of preserved rind from oranges, limes and sometimes pumpkin, ideal for adding flavour and texture to desserts.

CANNELLINI BEANS

Small, white kidney beans which should be soaked overnight before cooking.

CEDRO LEMON

A form of candied fruit rind.

CREME DE CASSIS

A sticky blackcurrant liqueur, best used as an additive for desserts. Bols is a reliable brand.

EGG (PLUM) TOMATOES

The shape for tomatoes favoured by Italians for making flavourful sauces.

ENGLISH SPINACH

This is the traditional form of spinach. Variants are silverbeet and Swiss chard, which we don't think work quite as well in most of these recipes.

GOAT'S CHEESE

A strong-flavoured cheese which comes in a hard form and a soft, creamy form. Our recipes always use the soft form.

LINGUINE

A thin form of spaghetti, slightly flattened.

MARSALA

A slightly sweet Sicilian wine similar to sherry. Not to be confused with egg marsala liqueur.

MASCARPONE

A soft creamy cheese which is so rich it is best used as a topping for desserts.

MIGNONETTE

A common form of green lettuce.

OLIVE OIL

Use the light version for cooking, and the extra virgin for dressings.

ORANGE BLOSSOM WATER

A highly aromatic flavouring to give desserts a touch of the Middle East. Available in most specialist food stores, particularly Lebanese delicatessens.

ORECCHIETTE

A pasta in the shape of little ears, originating in Italy's south east.

PANCETTA

A kind of bacon, but with a less smoky flavour.

PAPPARDELLE

Very wide, flat noodles, often used with game sauces.

POLENTA

Yellow corn meal that makes a savoury porridge, often used as an alternative to mashed potato.

PORCINI

Large powerfully-flavoured mushrooms which are usually sold dried.

PROSCIUTTO

A strong-flavoured form of ham, cured with salt and air dried.

PROVOLONE

A tasty semi-hard cheese, good for grilling.

RADICCHIO

A bitter-tasting red lettuce.

SAVOIARDI

Sweet airy biscuits, like sponge fingers.

STREGA OR GALLIANO

Strong-flavoured yellow liqueurs high in alcohol and flavoured with herbs to a secret formula.

VANILLA POWDER

The best way to give the sharp taste of vanilla to a dessert. The next best way is vanilla extract/essence. Never use vanilla sugar, which is too sweet.

ZABAGLIONE

A light confection of egg yolks and sugar, often flavoured with sweet alcohol or, for children, with diluted coffee.

General Recipes

Neapolitan Sauce

THIS RECIPE YIELDS ABOUT 2¹/₂ CUPS (20 FL OZ/600 ML)

2 lb/1 kg fresh cooking tomatoes or 1¹/₄ lb/600 g canned
  peeled tomatoes
5 tablespoons olive oil
3 cloves garlic, whole
10 basil leaves, chopped
salt to taste

If using fresh tomatoes, cut a cross in the skin at the
top, and drop tomatoes into a bowl of very hot water for
10 seconds. Pour off water, then peel skin off tomatoes.
Chop them.

Place olive oil and garlic in a large pan and fry until
garlic is golden, about 1 minute. Add chopped
tomatoes and basil. Simmer for 30 minutes. Add salt.

Transfer cooled sauce into sealed containers and store
in refrigerator. Ideally, the sauce should be used within
2 days of being made.

∽

Meat Stock

PRODUCES 4 CUPS (1 L) MEAT STOCK

3 tablespoons butter
3 oz/90 g carrots, chopped
4 oz/125 g onions, chopped
2 oz/60 g celery, chopped
1 lb/500 g inexpensive cut of beef, cubed
1 lb/500 g beef bones, preferably joints and legs
8 cups (2 l) red wine
6 bay leaves
20 peppercorns
1 bunch parsley, chopped
¹/₂ teaspoon salt
24 cups (6 l) water

Melt butter in a very large pan, and fry carrots, onions,
and celery for 5 minutes on high heat. Add beef and
bones, and cook for 10 minutes. Add wine, and simmer
for 10 minutes. Add bay leaves, peppercorns, and
parsley, salt, and water, and bring to a boil. Reduce heat
to low, and simmer, uncovered, for 8 hours. From time
to time, skim the scum off top.

Remove from heat and strain, keeping the stock.

For a heavier stock, simmer strained stock over low
heat for another hour.

∽

Basic Sponge

5 eggs, separated
5 oz/150 g sugar
1 1/4 cups (5 oz/150 g) plain (all-purpose) flour
grated rind of 1/2 lemon
1/4 teaspoon vanilla powder or extract (see glossary)
butter for greasing pan
flour for dusting

Preheat oven to 275°F (140°C/Gas 1).

Beat egg yolks with sugar until white and creamy. Slowly fold in flour. Add lemon rind and vanilla. Beat egg whites separately until stiff. Fold into yolk mixture.

Butter base and sides of an 8 inch/20 cm spring-base cake pan. Dust with flour. Pour in mixture. Bake for 20 minutes. Insert a skewer into the middle of the cake; if it comes out clean, the cake is cooked. If not, cook for a further 5 minutes.

∞

Basic Polenta

9 cups (2.25 l) water
5 bay leaves
13 oz/400 g polenta powder
pinch salt
polenta powder for dusting

TO MAKE SOFT POLENTA: Bring water to a boil with bay leaves. Slowly whisk in polenta powder. When all polenta has been added, reduce heat and simmer for 1 hour, stirring regularly with the whisk. If polenta starts to dry out, add a ladle of hot water. Remove bay leaves before serving.

TO MAKE GRILLED POLENTA: Pour soft polenta into a baking dish, and allow to cool and set. Cut into 2 inch/5 cm squares. Dust with raw polenta powder, and place on an oiled hotplate, in an oiled frying pan or under a heated grill (broiler). Cook until golden, about 5 minutes on both sides.

∞

Whipped Mascarpone

THIS RECIPE MAKES ABOUT 2 CUPS (16 FL OZ/500 ML)

4 eggs, separated
4 tablespoons sugar
1 lb/500 g mascarpone (see glossary)
6 tablespoons brandy
6 tablespoons strega liqueur or Galliano (see glossary)

Beat egg yolks with sugar. Blend with mascarpone at high speed in a blender or with lots of energetic beating by hand.

Whip egg whites separately until stiff, then gently stir into mascarpone mixture. Stir in brandy and liqueur. Refrigerate. Stir again before using, and serve chilled.

∞

Semifreddo

6 egg yolks
4 tablespoons sugar
4 1/2 cups (36 fl oz/1.125 l) cream (suitable for whipping)
2 tablespoons brandy
2 tablespoons dry marsala (not egg marsala liqueur)

Thoroughly blend egg yolks with sugar. Beat cream until fairly stiff and fold in the egg yolk mixture. Add brandy and marsala; stir well. Line a large and deep rectangular container (a baking dish, for example) with waxed (greaseproof) paper. Pour in cream mixture and freeze for at least 4 hours.

∞

Spring Menu One

SERVES 4

Finocchiara
FENNEL AND ARTICHOKE SALAD

~

Linguine with Pesto Sauce

~

Perch Puccini

~

Torta di Riso
RICE CAKES

~

The weather is warming up. Let's welcome spring with a beautifully balanced meal that opens with a salad, to get the digestive juices flowing. In the salad, let's use some powerful winter ingredients that linger into spring. The idea of eating raw artichoke may come as a surprise, but the Italians have been doing it for centuries (they pronounce the dish "fee-nock-ee-yara"). Use only the tender inner leaves, and soak them well with lemon and olive oil (extra virgin, of course). The result is a joyous mixture of textures and flavours.

We'll follow that with a very traditional pasta dish, covered with a basil sauce that is claimed by both Genoa in the north of Italy and Naples in the south. Italians like to make their pesto sauce in the summer and preserve it in long jars under olive oil right through the winter. They say it "matures" that way. Genoese sailors centuries ago took pesto sauce on their sea journeys, so it would not be unrealistic to assume that one long distance traveller who carried such a souvenir of his home port could have been Christopher Columbus. We're making our pesto fresh with the first basil leaves of spring. The recipe yields about 4 cups of sauce although only 1 cup is needed for the linguine—store the rest for later use.

After these two full-flavoured appetisers, the main course of fish steamed with wine is designed as a light contrast. Keeping to the spirit of simplicity, serve it with just steamed potatoes sprinkled with a little chopped parsley. That way your guests won't overload their palates before the spectacular dessert of rice cake with candied fruits, served with zabaglione. We've used arborio rice, which is the fat and fluffy kind, but if you can't find it, other types of white rice will still produce a rather luscious result.

Finocchiara

FENNEL AND ARTICHOKE SALAD

Linguine
with Pesto Sauce

2 fennel bulbs, washed well
3 globe artichokes, washed well
salt to taste
6 tablespoons extra virgin olive oil
3 tablespoons lemon juice
1¹/2 oz/50 g parmesan cheese
freshly ground black pepper to taste

Remove two outer layers of fennel bulbs and discard. Slice fennel finely.

Remove outer leaves of artichokes (about 12 of them) and discard. Chop off top third of artichokes and discard. Cut artichokes in half, and remove beards from the middle and discard. Slice artichoke very finely.

Mix fennel and artichoke in a bowl. Season with a little salt. Add oil and lemon juice, and mix well.

Place on serving plate. Pour juice from bowl on top. With a vegetable peeler, shave parmesan over the salad until well covered. Top with pepper.

∾

PESTO SAUCE:
4 tablespoons pine nuts
1 bunch fresh basil
5 tablespoons freshly grated parmesan cheese
2 cloves garlic, chopped
6 tablespoons extra virgin olive oil
salt and freshly ground black pepper to taste

9 oz/280 g linguine (see glossary)
freshly grated parmesan cheese
extra pine nuts for garnish (optional)

First make the pesto sauce. Preheat oven to 350°F (180°C/Gas 4). Roast pine nuts on a baking sheet until they begin to brown, about 3 minutes. Remove all stems from basil, and brush leaves with a damp cloth. Place basil leaves, pine nuts, parmesan, and garlic in a blender or food processor. Process on high speed, dribbling in olive oil. Add salt and pepper.

Boil linguine for about 7 minutes. Drain.

Place 1 cup pesto sauce in a large bowl, add pasta, and mix. Divide into four serving bowls, and sprinkle with parmesan. Garnish with extra pine nuts, and serve immediately.

∾

Perch Puccini

2 cloves garlic, minced

1¹/2 cups (12 fl oz/375 ml) olive oil

4 fillets perch, about 10 oz/315 g each, cleaned

8 oz/250 g button mushrooms (champignons), finely sliced

1 bottle dry white wine

2 tablespoons lemon juice

4 tablespoons finely chopped parsley

Add garlic to oil and let stand for 1¹/2 hours.

Preheat oven to 400°F (200°C/Gas 6).

Cover fish with mushroom pieces so that they look like scales. Place a wire rack in a baking dish, and pour in wine until it reaches just below the rack. Place fish with mushrooms on the rack, cover dish with foil, and bake for 18 minutes.

Transfer pieces of fish to separate serving plates.

Add lemon juice and parsley to olive oil and garlic mixture. Stir briskly, and pour over fish.

Serve with steamed potatoes sprinkled with parsley.

Torta di Riso

····································

RICE CAKES

7 oz/220 g arborio rice (see glossary)

7 cups (1.75 l) milk

2 oz/60 g sugar

4 oz/125 g candied fruit (see glossary)

salt

5 eggs, separated

4 tablespoons orange blossom water (see glossary)

4 tablespoons orange liqueur (eg Grand Marnier)

about 3 tablespoons unsalted butter

5 tablespoons dry fine breadcrumbs

Preheat oven to 330°F (175°C/Gas 3).

Simmer rice and milk in a saucepan for 15 minutes, stirring frequently. Remove from heat. Add sugar, candied fruit, and a pinch of salt. Stir, then allow to cool.

Add egg yolks to cooled rice mixture and stir. Add orange blossom water and liqueur. Mix well.

Beat egg whites with a pinch of salt till stiff. Fold gently into rice mixture.

Butter four 2½ inch/6 cm cake moulds and dust with breadcrumbs. Shake off any excess. Spoon mixture into moulds. Sprinkle with breadcrumbs, and add a small dob of butter on top. Bake until light brown on top and a skewer inserted in the middle comes out dry, about 15 minutes. Remove from moulds: run a knife around the outer edge, turn mould upside down and pat base gently. Serve cold with zabaglione (see recipe on page 145).

Spring Menu Two

SERVES 4

Zuppa di Verdure

VEGETABLE SOUP

∿

Insalata Fantasia

ROAST PORK AND MUSHROOM SALAD

∿

Pollo al Rosmarino

ROSEMARY CHICKEN

∿

Fettuccine con Pomodoro

STRAWBERRY "PASTA"

∿

H ere's a menu for one of those early spring days when a winter chill continues to linger, and your guests will appreciate the warmth of a hearty soup. This soup is a classic, crammed with healthy ingredients, as well as wine and cream for a touch of decadence. Roast pork and mushrooms are equally comforting fare for early spring days, but we're serving the pork at room temperature, and cutting its heaviness with radicchio, the wonderfully sharp red lettuce that is used with devotion in the northeast of Italy, near Venice. "The king of salads" they call it, and we must agree. We'll celebrate radicchio again in our autumn and winter menus.

Along with basil, rosemary is our favourite herb, and it is ideal to give a tang to the combination of chicken and tomatoes in our main course. This is a juicy dish, so soak up the sauce with rice or mashed potato.

Yes, we admit it, the dessert is a joke. A visual pun lends this dish its name. Fettuccine con pomodoro literally means "pasta with tomato", because that's how it looks. In reality, slices of thin pancake with strawberry sauce are sprinkled with chocolate, which simulates ground pepper, and mint, simulating parsley. That's what we mean about Italians liking to have fun with their food. By the way, it tastes great, and if you have any reservations about such a rich dessert, just think how healthy you've been for the rest of the meal.

∾

Zuppa di Verdure

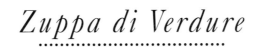

VEGETABLE SOUP

2 tablespoons olive oil

2 tablespoons butter

1 brown onion, coarsely chopped

2 leeks, coarsely chopped

8 oz/250 g carrots, coarsely chopped

2 potatoes, coarsely chopped

1¹/2 stalks celery, coarsely chopped

1 cup (8 fl oz/250 ml) dry white wine

3 cups (24 fl oz/750 ml) light chicken stock
    (commercial or homemade)

1 cup (8 fl oz/250 ml) light (single) cream

salt

¹/4 bunch parsley, chopped

Heat oil and butter in a large saucepan over medium high heat, and fry onion and leeks until soft, about 1 minute. Stir in carrots and cook for 4 minutes. Add potatoes, and cook for 5 minutes, stirring from time to time. Add celery, and cook for 3 minutes. Add white wine and 2 cups stock, and cook over medium heat for 15 minutes.

Puree in a blender or food processor, and return to pan. Add remaining stock, cream, and a pinch of salt. Bring to just below boiling point, then serve, sprinkled with parsley

∞

Insalata Fantasia

....

ROAST PORK AND MUSHROOM SALAD

9 oz/280 g pork fillet

1 egg

1 tablespoon freshly grated parmesan cheese

salt and freshly ground black pepper to taste

¹/₂ clove garlic, minced

4 tablespoons olive oil

4 oz/125 g button mushrooms (champignons), sliced

2 rashers bacon, chopped

2 mignonette lettuces (see glossary)

1 radicchio lettuce (see glossary)

Preheat oven to 350°F (180°C/Gas 4).

With a knife, make a hole down the centre of the pork fillet for about three-quarters of its length. Beat together egg, parmesan, salt, pepper, and garlic, and stuff mixture into the fillet. Close and tie with string. Place 2 tablespoons oil and pork in a baking dish, and bake for 1 hour. Remove from oven, and allow to rest for 2 hours.

Heat 2 tablespoons oil in a frying pan and sauté mushrooms and bacon for 5 minutes.

Arrange mignonette and radicchio leaves on plates, and sprinkle with mushrooms and bacon. Slice cooled pork thinly and arrange on top. Season to taste.

∾

Pollo al Rosmarino

....

ROSEMARY CHICKEN

3¹/₂ lb/1.75 kg chicken

6 tablespoons olive oil

1 brown onion, chopped

2 cloves garlic, minced

4 tablespoons plain (all-purpose) flour

6 sage leaves, chopped

1 teaspoon chopped fresh rosemary

1¹/₂ cups (12 fl oz/375 ml) red wine

14 oz/440 g can tomatoes, chopped

Preheat oven to 350°F (180°C/Gas 4). Cut chicken into four pieces. Wash and dry with cloth.

Place oil in baking dish, add onion, and fry on stove over medium high heat until soft, about 1 minute. Add garlic, and fry for a further minute.

Dust chicken with flour. Add to baking dish with sage and rosemary. Brown chicken on both sides for 2 minutes. Add wine, and cook for 2 minutes over medium high heat to reduce wine. Add tomatoes. Bake in oven for 30 minutes.

Serve with white rice or mashed potato.

∾

Fettuccine con Pomodoro

STRAWBERRY "PASTA"

PANCAKE MIXTURE:

2 eggs
1 cup (4 oz/125 g) plain (all-purpose) flour
pinch salt
1 cup (8 fl oz/250 ml) milk
2 tablespoons butter
1 tablespoon sugar
butter for frying

STRAWBERRY SAUCE:

14 oz/440 g strawberries, hulled
3 tablespoons sugar
4 tablespoons maraschino or cherry liqueur

TOPPING:

block of white chocolate
mint leaves for garnish

First make the pancake mixture. Place eggs, flour, and salt in a bowl, and whisk together well. Stir in milk. Melt butter and sugar over low heat, and add to mixture. Mix vigorously until it forms a smooth paste. Leave to stand for 30 minutes.

Smear a nonstick frying pan with butter, warm pan over high heat for 30 seconds, then remove from heat and pour in enough pancake mixture to cover the surface thinly. Return to heat and cook for 10 seconds until golden, then flip pancake over and cook the other side for 10 seconds. Turn out onto a plate, and repeat the procedure until all the mixture has been used and you have a stack of pancakes.

Slice pancakes into fine strips resembling fettuccine.

Puree strawberries in blender or food processor with sugar and liqueur. Pour into saucepan and simmer for 5 minutes over low heat.

Arrange pancake strips in birds' nest shapes on separate serving plates. Pour strawberry sauce into the middle of each nest. Use a vegetable peeler to shave chocolate over the top. Garnish with mint leaves.

Spring Menu Three

SERVES 4

Gamberi con Fagioli

PRAWNS WITH BEANS

❧

Cotolette alla Pompeano

PORK WITH RED CABBAGE

❧

Frutta Gratinata

BAKED FRUIT

❧

The combination of seafood and beans is unusual in traditional Italian cooking—even in Tuscany where the people are obsessed with beans—and it would never have happened before this adventurous century. Thankfully, some genius discovered that a blend of large prawns and the small beans called fagioli ("fadj-o-lee") is a marriage made in heaven, especially when sealed with extra virgin olive oil and ground pepper. Try to use fresh prawns—frozen ones tend to be tough.

Our main course, from northern Italy where some of the cooking has Austrian elements, sounds wintry but works perfectly well as spring moves towards its peak. The olive paste adds a splash of the Mediterranean, and the whole package is visually exciting: gold cutlets, crimson cabbage and the black of olive paste. The name we've given it may sound as if its secrets were buried under a volcano, but in fact "rosso pompeano" is a deep red colour not unlike our cabbage, used in the ancient frescoes of many cities including Pompei. If you crave green to complete the portrait, try an arugola salad on the side.

The dessert, frutta gratinata, a glorification of this season's abundance, is an attempt to bring together as many newly ripened fruits as you can get your hands on. In summer, you might eat these fruits raw, but in spring it's still cool enough to cook them into a rich stew with a crunchy topping. If you insist on pure health, you could leave the Grand Marnier liqueur out of the sauce. But hey, this is a celebration.

∾

Gamberi con Fagioli

....

PRAWNS WITH BEANS

7 oz/220 g cannellini beans (see glossary)

2 bay leaves

1/2 stalk celery, chopped

1/2 onion, chopped

10 peppercorns

16 green king prawns (jumbo shrimp)

1 clove garlic, chopped

2 tablespoons olive oil

2 egg (plum) tomatoes, diced

8 arugola (rocket) leaves, coarsely chopped (see glossary)

4 teaspoons extra virgin olive oil

Soak beans overnight with bay leaves in a saucepan in water to cover.

Add celery, onion, and peppercorns. Bring to a boil, and simmer for 20 minutes. Strain beans, removing bay leaves and peppercorns but saving the cooking water, and set aside.

Cook prawns for 5 minutes in boiling water and peel.

Place garlic and 2 tablespoons olive oil in frying pan and fry over medium high heat for 30 seconds. Add beans and stir. Add 1/2 cup of cooking water and prawns. Heat through, about 2 minutes.

Place prawn and bean mixture on serving plates. Sprinkle with tomato and arugola. Drizzle 1 teaspoon extra virgin olive oil over each plate.

Cotolette alla Pompeano

PORK WITH RED CABBAGE

2 eggs

2 tablespoons grated parmesan cheese

3 tablespoons chopped fresh rosemary

salt and freshly ground black pepper to taste

8 pork cutlets (chops)

about 5 tablespoons plain (all-purpose) flour

2 oz/60 g coarse fresh breadcrumbs

$^1/_2$ clove garlic, minced

2 tablespoons olive oil

$^1/_3$ red cabbage (about 12 oz/375 g), shredded

about 6 tablespoons dry white wine

5 tablespoons white wine vinegar

6 oz/180 g butter

8 teaspoons olive paste (commercial)

Beat eggs with parmesan, rosemary, salt and pepper. Dust pork with flour, dip into egg mixture, and coat with breadcrumbs.

Place garlic and oil in frying pan and fry over medium high heat until garlic is golden, about 30 seconds. Add cabbage and toss for 1 minute. Add wine, and simmer over medium heat for 10 minutes. Add vinegar, and cook for 8 minutes. If mixture dries out, add extra wine. Season to taste.

Melt some of the butter in a large nonstick frying pan. Fry pork, a few pieces at a time, for about 6 minutes on each side over medium heat, or until golden. Add more butter for each new batch.

Serve pork topped with 1 teaspoon olive paste on each piece, and surrounded by red cabbage. Accompany with an arugola salad.

Frutta Gratinata

BAKED FRUIT

1 bunch rhubarb, chopped

2 tablespoons water

2 tablespoons butter

2 tablespoons sugar

1¹/₂ cups (12 fl oz/375 ml) orange juice

2 apples, cubed

2 pears, cubed

1 banana, cubed

7 oz/220 g strawberries, hulled and cubed

1 cup (8 oz/250 ml) orange liqueur (eg Grand Marnier)

8 amaretti biscuits (see glossary)

2 oz/60 g unsalted pistachio nuts, shelled

4 tablespoons double (heavy) cream

Steam rhubarb with water in a tightly lidded saucepan for 20 minutes over low heat.

Preheat oven to 350°F (180°C/Gas 4).

Cook butter and sugar in a frying pan over high heat until they begin to caramelise, about 2 minutes. Add orange juice and stir for 1 minute. Add all fruit, except rhubarb, and cook over medium heat for 3 minutes, stirring frequently. Remove from heat.

Stir in liqueur and rhubarb. Place mixture in soufflé dish, about 5 inches/12 cm in diameter, 2 inches/5 cm deep. Crush amaretti and pistachios either in a blender or with a rolling pin. Sprinkle on top of fruit mixture. Bake for 10 minutes. Serve with cream.

Spring Menu Four

SERVES 4

Seafood Lasagna

~

Agnello Primavera

ROAST LAMB WITH SWEET POTATO PUREE

~

Cassata Siciliana

~

I t's time for a little more seafood and a little less convention. Here we've used it to ring some changes on an old standard—lasagna. The classic lasagna, which has been a favourite since the time of the ancient Romans (who called it laganum), consists of dense meat sauce sandwiched between multiple sheets of pasta and covered with cheese. Sometimes it is cooked for so long it consolidates into a kind of brick. Well, for spring, we have lightened it up. Our pasta is draped rather than crammed onto the sauce, in a style increasingly fashionable in the north of Italy. And there's no cheese to overwhelm the delicate seafood flavours. Your guests should have plenty of appetite left for the next two courses.

Italians believe lamb (pronounced "an-yello") is the sweetest meat to eat in spring, flavoured, of course, with red wine and rosemary. Here it is combined with the lusciousness of sweet potato, sharpened slightly with sage. We also suggest a salad of dark green, peppery arugola leaves with a splash of olive oil, to freshen up the tastebuds before dessert.

And now for another twist on a classic. Cassata is a traditional Sicilian Easter dish, and it's usually wrapped in dense marzipan icing, which makes it heavy and very sweet. Our modification retains the essential elements—ricotta and candied fruit—but leaves you with plenty of verve so you can take that walk in the fresh spring air.

∞

Seafood Lasagna

6 small calamari (squid)

2 cloves garlic, crushed

3 tablespoons olive oil

2 cups (16 fl oz/500 ml) dry white wine

20 mussels, in their shells

20 small clams (vongole), in their shells

2 tablespoons butter

1 leek, chopped

20 small green prawns (shrimp), peeled

1 cup (8 fl oz/250 ml) light (single) cream

salt and freshly ground black pepper to taste

16 sheets green lasagna

Clean calamari, remove ink sacs, separate tentacles from bodies, and cut bodies into rings.

Fry 1 crushed garlic clove in 2 tablespoons olive oil in a frying pan over medium heat for 30 seconds. Add rings and tentacles, and fry for 2¹/₂ minutes.

Add 1 cup wine. Cook for 20 minutes over medium heat, adding more wine if calamari starts to dry out.

In a casserole pot, fry remaining garlic in remaining olive oil for 30 seconds. Add mussels, clams, and remaining wine. Cook until shells open, about 5 minutes. Discard any that do not open. Remove mussels and clams from their shells and discard shells. Strain sauce very finely to remove any grit or bits of shell. Place mussels and clams back in sauce.

Melt butter in a frying pan, and fry leek for 1 minute. Add prawns and toss. Add cooked calamari in its sauce and mussels and clams in their sauce. Simmer for 3 minutes. Add cream, and simmer for 5 minutes. Season with salt and pepper.

Boil lasagna according to the instructions on the pack (usually about 7 minutes). Place one sheet of pasta on each plate, and cover with seafood sauce. Place another sheet irregularly over that, cover again with sauce, and continue for the other two sheets. Top with remaining sauce.

Agnello Primavera

ROAST LAMB WITH SWEET POTATO PUREE

4 small racks of lamb (4 to 6 cutlets/chops per rack)

5 tablespoons plain (all-purpose) flour

4 tablespoons vegetable oil

4 stems fresh rosemary

4 cloves garlic

1 bottle red wine

1 lb/500 g sweet potatoes or yams, peeled

2 tablespoons butter

2 teaspoons chopped fresh sage

1 cup (8 fl oz/250 ml) meat stock (commercial, or see recipe on page 12), warmed

Preheat oven to 400°F (200°C/Gas 6).

Dust lamb with flour. In a baking dish, place oil, rosemary, garlic, and lamb. Roast lamb for 1 minute each side. Remove from oven, and pour off most of the oil. Fill pan with wine up to about three-quarters of its depth. Return to oven and cook for 13 minutes. Turn lamb, and cook for another 3 minutes. Lamb will be pink to light brown. For well-done lamb, cook for another 5 minutes. Remove from oven and allow to rest for 2 minutes before slicing into individual cutlets.

Meanwhile, cover sweet potatoes with water in a saucepan and boil until soft, about 20 minutes. Place in a bowl with butter and sage, and mash. For a smoother texture, puree in a blender or food processor.

Place a mound of sweet potato in the middle of each serving plate, and surround it with lamb, bones pointing towards the middle. Spoon 3 tablespoons of warmed stock over each serving. Accompany with arugola salad.

Cassata Siciliana

1 sponge, bought or homemade (see recipe on page 13)

6 tablespoons crème de cassis liqueur (see glossary)

6 tablespoons water

1¹/₄ cups (10 oz/300 g) sugar

1¹/₂ lb/750 g ricotta cheese

2 oz/50 g candied fruit, diced (see glossary)

2 oz/50 g sultanas (golden raisins)

2 oz/50 g dark cooking (semi-sweet) chocolate, finely chopped

2 oz/50 g unsalted pistachio nuts, shelled

about 3 tablespoons brandy

about 3 tablespoons strega liqueur (see glossary)

Preheat oven to 350°F (180°C/Gas 4).

Slice sponge thinly, about ¹/₄ inch/5 mm thick. Layer bottom and sides of an 11-inch/28 cm diameter spring-form cake pan with sponge. Brush with crème de cassis.

In a saucepan, bring water to a boil, add sugar, and simmer until syrup starts to thicken, about 15 minutes. Allow syrup to cool, and mix into ricotta, using a whisk. Add candied fruit, sultanas, and chocolate, and mix well.

Roast pistachio nuts on baking sheet in oven until they look golden and smell roasted, about 3 minutes. Grind nuts coarsely. Add half the ground nuts to ricotta mixture. Add brandy and strega to taste.

Fill the sponge-lined cake pan with mixture; and sprinkle remaining ground nuts over the top. Place in freezer for 4 hours. Remove 1 hour before serving.

SERVES 4

Bruschetta

~

*Spaghetti with
Mussels and Clams*

~

Involtini

VEAL ROLLS WITH EMMENTHAL AND CABBAGE

~

*Poached Peaches with
Amaretti Biscuits*

~

I talians love to titillate their palates as a meal begins, and the simplest way to do this is with bruschetta (pronounced "broo-sketta"), which we could translate unromantically into English as tomatoes on toast. To do it justice, you should use the right kind of tomatoes, fully ripe, and allow long enough for them to become steeped in basil, oil, and garlic. Your choice of dense crusty bread is also important. Then your only problem will be stopping your guests from eating too many.

Every Italian seaport has its own version of spaghetti with shellfish, and this is how we might enjoy it in Naples or Sicily. The chillies are optional, but they give the dish a marvellous lift and you can vary the quantity to your taste.

After that burst of Mediterranean sunshine, your palate will welcome the gentler flavour of the involtini. The meat should be young and tender, so that it won't dry and toughen in the heat once it has been rolled around the cabbage, ham, and cheese. We're accompanying the veal rolls with borlotti beans, which are as healthy as they are toothsome.

The delicacy of the dessert is designed to contrast with the peasant-style main course. It has a very refined flavour, and both soft and crunchy textures from the peach flesh and the amaretti biscuits. Peaches begin to appear in late spring, and here's your excuse to make great use of this delectable fruit.

∞

Bruschetta

Spaghetti with Mussels and Clams

10 egg (plum) tomatoes
6 basil leaves, chopped
6 tablespoons olive oil
1 clove garlic, minced
salt and freshly ground black pepper to taste
12 slices dense Italian bread, 1 day old

Cut a cross into skin at top of plum tomatoes, and drop them into boiling water for 10 seconds. Remove from water, peel off skin, and dice flesh.

Mix basil with olive oil, garlic, and salt and pepper. Add to tomatoes. Set aside for 1 hour.

Toast bread. Top each piece of toast with about 1 tablespoon tomato mixture and serve immediately.

∾

24 mussels
24 small clams (vongole)
7 tablespoons olive oil
6 cloves garlic, whole
2 small, dried red chillies (optional)
3 cups (24 fl oz/750 ml) dry white wine
9 oz/280 g spaghetti
4 tablespoons chopped parsley

Scrub mussel and clam shells, removing stalks and beards from mussels.

Place olive oil, garlic, and chillies into a very large frying pan, or two smaller frying pans, over high heat. Fry until garlic is golden, about 1 minute. Add mussels and clams, and cook until shells open, about 5 minutes. Discard any that do not open. Remove top halves of shells. Add wine. Cook for another 10 minutes.

Meanwhile, boil spaghetti, about 7 minutes. Drain, and add to the frying pan. Toss mixture, divide into four serving bowls, and sprinkle with parsley.

∾

Involtini

....

VEAL ROLLS WITH EMMENTHAL AND CABBAGE

8 oz/250 g borlotti beans (see glossary)

3 bay leaves

2 cloves garlic, squashed

8 cabbage leaves

*8 thin slices veal fillet, about 6 x 4 inches/15 x 10 cm
    and 1/4 inch/5 mm thick*

8 thin slices pancetta (see glossary) or bacon

8 slices emmenthal cheese or other mild Swiss cheese

about 4 tablespoons plain (all-purpose) flour

1 small brown onion, chopped

4 tablespoons olive oil

*2 cups (16 fl oz/500 ml) meat stock (commercial,
    or see recipe on page 12)*

salt and freshly ground black pepper to taste

Soak beans overnight with bay leaves and garlic in plenty of water. Bring beans to a boil, reduce heat, and simmer for 1 hour. Drain. Remove bay leaves and garlic.

Dip cabbage into boiling water and remove immediately. Dry and place one leaf on top of each piece of veal, then add one slice of pancetta and one slice of cheese. Roll veal into a cylinder and secure with toothpicks. Dust with flour.

Place onion and oil in a flame-proof casserole pot over medium heat and fry until onion is soft, about 3 minutes. Add veal rolls and brown for 1 minute. Add 1 cup meat stock and bring to a boil. Add beans. Reduce heat, add remaining stock and simmer until sauce thickens, about 7 minutes. Season with salt and pepper.

Remove veal rolls and discard toothpicks. Place rolls on serving plates and pour sauce over the top.

Poached Peaches with Amaretti Biscuits

16 amaretti biscuits (see glossary)

2 tablespoons unsalted butter

3 tablespoons amaretto liqueur (see glossary)

4 firm peaches, peeled, halved and pitted

1 bottle dry white wine

5 cloves

1/4 cinnamon stick

4 tablespoons sugar

crushed amaretti biscuits for garnish

Preheat oven to 350° F (180°C/Gas 4).

Crush amaretti biscuits to form a coarse flour, either in a food processor or with a rolling pin.

Soften butter in a saucepan over low heat. In a bowl, mix butter with crushed amaretti and a third of the liqueur until smooth. Fill each peach half with this mixture.

Place a wire rack in a baking dish. Pour wine into the dish until it reaches just below the rack. Add cloves and cinnamon stick to wine. Place peaches on rack, and cover dish with foil. Bake for 15 minutes.

Transfer peaches to serving plates. Strain juice from baking dish, and pour half into a saucepan. Add sugar and remaining liqueur, bring to a boil, and stir until liquid thickens. Pour over peaches. Garnish the plates with crushed amaretti, if desired

Summer Menu One

Antipasto of
Stuffed Eggplant
& Capsicums with
Anchovy Dressing

∾

Calamari with
Olive Paste

∾

Beef with Salsa Verde

∾

Semifreddo with
Prunes

∾

I t's the season for the long and leisurely lunch, drifting from one light, tasty course to the next via wine and conversation. And, to an Italian, the natural opening for a leisurely lunch is antipasto. Some Italian restaurants in English-speaking countries have tried to kid us that antipasto consists of a few slices of cold meat and processed cheese. This is akin to trying to tickle the mouth with a sledgehammer instead of a feather. In Italian homes, antipasto is more likely to be vegetables, occasionally enhanced with a little meat or fish as a sauce.

Our antipasto, on this occasion, involves eggplant and capsicum, both symbolic of the sunny Mediterranean. Be sure to spoon lots of the olive sauce over the eggplant after you slice it. And a hint about the capsicum: we've suggested you cook it in the oven, but if you have a gas stove, a more entertaining way to give it a barbecued flavour is to light a gas jet and simply sit the capsicum on it, turning the capsicum occasionally with tongs, until the skin is entirely blackened. The process should take no more than 5 minutes. Then strip the skin off and slice the capsicum as the recipe suggests. You'll be surprised how sweet the "burned" flesh tastes.

Having thus stimulated our appetites, we retain the Mediterranean mood with an appetiser of baby calamari with olive paste. Allow a few minutes break before serving the main course, which is rare beef with one of the great Italian classic sauces. Salsa verde is deceptively easy to make —you just throw all the ingredients into a blender and whiz. But the complex chemistry which takes place produces a condiment for meat which far outdoes Anglo Saxon favourites such as mustard or horseradish.

Our final indulgence is a semifreddo (literally "half-cold"), an easy version of icecream. Semifreddo can have all sorts of fruit fillings, but we've chosen prunes lightened by a little lemon rind, because that creates both a sweetness and a refreshing sharpness.

Stuffed Eggplant

1 large eggplant (aubergine)

1 ripe tomato

1 bocconcini (see glossary)

6 tablespoons extra virgin olive oil

1/2 Spanish (purple) onion, chopped

6 black olives, pitted

1 tablespoon capers, soaked in water for 30 minutes
  then drained

1 teaspoon dried oregano

salt to taste

Preheat oven to 350°F (180°C/Gas 4).

Make four deep grooves in the side of eggplant, equally spaced along its length. Slice tomato and bocconcini each into four pieces, and insert a piece of each into each groove of eggplant.

Place oil and onion in a baking dish. Place eggplant on top. Cover dish with foil and bake in oven for 30 minutes.

Remove foil. Add olives and capers, and baste eggplant with the mixture. Sprinkle with oregano and a little salt. Cover again with foil, and bake for another 15 minutes.

Slice into four before serving, spooning olive sauce over. Can be served cold.

Capsicums with Anchovy Dressing

2 large red capsicums (bell peppers)

4 anchovies, roughly chopped

1 clove garlic, crushed

5 tablespoons extra virgin olive oil

1 teaspoon balsamic vinegar (see glossary)
   or red wine vinegar

Preheat oven to 400°F (200°C/Gas 6).

Roast capsicums on top shelf of oven until skin wrinkles and starts to lift, about 20 minutes. Remove from oven, allow to cool, and strip off skin. Remove stalk and seeds, and slice into pieces about 1¹/₂ inches/ 3.5 cm wide. Place in a serving dish.

Mix remaining ingredients together, and pour over capsicums.

Calamari with Olive Paste

20 small calamari (squid), bodies only

28 snow peas (mange-tout)

3 teaspoons olive oil

2 cloves garlic, minced

1 cup (8 fl oz/250 ml) light meat stock (commercial, or see recipe on page 12)

16 cherry tomatoes

4 teaspoons black olive paste (commercial)

salt and freshly ground black pepper to taste

8 basil leaves, chopped

Add calamari to a saucepan of boiling water and simmer for 20 minutes, drain, and allow to cool.

Add snow peas to a saucepan of boiling water and boil for 1 minute, then plunge them into cold water for 1 minute, drain, and set aside.

Place oil and garlic in a frying pan over medium heat and fry for 30 seconds. Add calamari, and toss in oil for 1 minute. Add stock, and simmer for 10 minutes. Add tomatoes, olive paste, and a little salt and pepper. Turn heat to high, and toss for 1 minute.

Arrange seven snow peas in a star pattern on each plate. Arrange five calamari over the snow peas, and four tomatoes in the middle of each plate. Pour remaining sauce over calamari; sprinkle with basil. Serve warm.

Beef with Salsa Verde

1 piece fillet steak, about 1¹/₄ lb/625 g, trimmed

4 rashers bacon

1 tablespoon olive oil

2 carrots

1 leek

4 tablespoons plain (all-purpose) flour

4 cups (1 l) vegetable oil

SALSA VERDE:

1 large bunch parsley, chopped

1 medium potato, boiled and skinned

1 tablespoon capers, soaked in water for 30 minutes then drained

4 anchovies, chopped

1 tablespoon white wine vinegar

1¹/₂ tablespoons chopped onions

¹/₂ clove garlic, chopped

salt and freshly ground black pepper to taste

3 tablespoons olive oil

Preheat oven to 425°F (220°C/Gas 7).

Wrap bacon slices around beef. Tie with string.

Pour olive oil into a baking dish or a nonstick frying pan with an oven-proof handle. Add beef. Bake for 10 minutes, then turn beef and cook for another 10 minutes.

While beef is cooking, make the salsa verde by placing all ingredients except olive oil in a blender or food processor. Process, slowly adding oil, until mixture forms a smooth paste.

Remove beef from oven, and discard bacon. Allow to stand for 10 minutes.

While meat is resting, very finely slice carrots and leek into strips about 1 inch/2.5 cm long, and dust with flour. Discard any excess flour. Heat vegetable oil in a frying pan until very hot, and fry carrots and leeks until golden and crisp, about 3 minutes.

Slice meat into ¹/₄ inch/5 mm thick pieces. Place five slices in a circular arrangement on each plate. Spoon 1¹/₂ tablespoons of salsa verde onto the middle of each plate. Place hot carrot and leek chips on top, and serve.

Semifreddo with Prunes

24 prunes, pitted

2 1/2 cups (20 fl oz/625 ml) water

1/2 lemon

6 egg yolks

1 1/4 cups (10 oz/310 g) sugar

4 1/2 cups (36 fl oz/1.125 l) single (light) cream

2 oz/60 g unsalted pistachio nuts, shelled and chopped

5 amaretti biscuits, crushed (see glossary)

6 tablespoons brandy

3 cups (24 fl oz/750 ml) water

extra pistachio nuts to garnish (optional)

Gently simmer prunes in 2 1/2 cups water for 1 hour in a large pan with lemon and 3/4 cup sugar. Allow to cool. Discard lemon, separate prunes and juice, and set aside.

Thoroughly blend egg yolks with 1/4 cup sugar. Beat cream until fairly stiff and fold in egg yolk mixture. Then fold in pistachio nuts, amaretti, and brandy.

Line a large and deep rectangular container (a baking dish, for example) with waxed (greaseproof) paper. Pour in about a third of the cream mixture. Layer mixture with about half the prunes. Pour in another third of the cream mixture, and create another layer of prunes. Cover with the rest of the cream mixture. Freeze for at least 4 hours. You have created a semifreddo.

In a saucepan, add 3 cups water and remaining sugar to the prune juice. Reduce over medium heat for 10 minutes so that it forms a syrup. Allow to cool.

When you are ready to serve dessert, pour a little syrup in a half-moon shape on each plate. Then remove semifreddo from freezer and from its container, and slice into squares (or whatever shapes please you). Put one slice on each plate. Decorate with pistachio nuts.

Summer Menu Two

SERVES 4

Spaghetti Tricolore

SPAGHETTI WITH TOMATOES AND ARUGOLA

∾

Quaglie del Cardinale

QUAILS WITH CHERRIES

∾

Pesche nel Tempio

"TEMPLES" WITH PEACH PUREE

∾

his menu is a shameless display of patriotism for all things Italian, and a celebration of the colours of the season's newest produce. It begins with the Italian flag, which is called a "tricolore" because it is red, white, and green. So is our appetiser: the red of tomatoes, the white of the pasta, and the deep green of arugola. Of course, these days you can get tomatoes all year round, and we often hear laments about how tomatoes have become tough and tasteless. Much of the time they've been artificially ripened, and under those circumstances you'd do better to buy canned ones. Only in summer can you be confident of fresh tomatoes that are genuinely ripe and full of flavour.

Our main course is named after the deep crimson robes of an Italian cardinal, because of the cherries surrounding the quail and in the stuffing. Cherries have their brief moment of glory in high summer, and we think this is an exciting dish because the flavour combination of quail, bacon and cherries creates a "sweet and sour" effect. We'd suggest white rice or mashed potato as an unobtrusive accompaniment.

Pesche nel Tempio, our name for the dessert, translates literally as "peaches in the temple". It involves building your own miniature Roman temple out of sponge finger biscuits and toffee, and filling it with pureed peaches and icecream. The glorious golden colour is another seasonal sensation, as visually delightful as it is delicious.

∾

Spaghetti Tricolore

SPAGHETTI WITH TOMATOES AND ARUGOLA

16 egg (plum) tomatoes, halved

2 cloves garlic, chopped

6 tablespoons olive oil

9 oz/280 g spaghetti

1 bunch arugola (rocket), chopped coarsely (see glossary)

salt and freshly ground black pepper to taste

Preheat oven to 350°F (180°C/Gas 4).

Place tomatoes in a baking dish. Scatter garlic and spoon oil on top. Bake for 7 minutes.

Meanwhile, boil spaghetti in a large pot of water, about 7 minutes. Drain.

Remove baking dish from oven, and place over a low heat on the stove. Add spaghetti to tomatoes, and toss well. Stir in arugola, add salt and pepper, and serve without cooking arugola.

Quaglie del Cardinale

....

QUAILS WITH CHERRIES

16 fresh cherries, pitted

2 teaspoons grated fresh ginger

7 oz/220 g prosciutto (see glossary) or bacon, diced

8 quails, cleaned and dried

16 thin slices prosciutto or bacon

3 tablespoons olive oil

2 teaspoons minced garlic

3 cups (24 fl oz/750 ml) dry white wine

2 cups (16 fl oz/500 ml) light meat stock (commercial, or see recipe on page 12)

1/2 teaspoon butter (optional)

extra cherries for garnish

Preheat oven to 350°F (180°C/Gas 4).

Mix cherries, ginger, and diced prosciutto together, and stuff mixture into quails. Wrap two slices prosciutto around the breast of each quail, and secure with toothpicks. Tie quail legs together with string so the stuffing doesn't fall out.

Heat oil in a large baking dish over medium heat on stove. Add garlic and quails and fry for 2 minutes or until skin is browned, turning quails once. Add wine, and bake uncovered in oven for 10 minutes.

Remove from oven, turn quails, and add stock. Bake for another 10 minutes.

Place quails on serving plates, removing toothpicks and string. Pour sauce from baking dish over them. If sauce seems too thin, add 1/2 teaspoon butter and stir over medium heat on stove for 2 minutes. Garnish each plate with a couple of cherries. Accompany with white rice or mashed potato.

Pesche nel Tempio

"Temples" with Peach Puree

3 tablespoons water

5 oz/155 g sugar

16 savoiardi biscuits (see glossary) or sponge fingers

8 large or 10 small peaches

1 bottle sweet wine

1/4 stick cinnamon

2 tablespoons peach liqueur

8 scoops vanilla icecream

8 mint leaves

Preheat oven to 400°F (200°C/Gas 6).

Boil water and sugar in a saucepan until mixture thickens and starts to form toffee, about 10 minutes. Set aside for 2 minutes.

Slice savoiardi in half lengthwise, and lay two of the halves parallel (like railroad tracks) on waxed (greaseproof) paper. Put a dab of toffee on each end of each half, then lay two more halves across them, so that you have a square. Add another two slices across them, and then another two across, sticking them together with toffee, as if you are building a log cabin. Make three more baskets, each using eight savoiardi halves.

Place peaches on a wire rack in baking dish, and pour in enough wine to fill to just under rack. Add cinnamon stick to wine, cover with foil, and bake for 12 minutes. Let peaches cool, then remove skins and seeds. Puree peaches in a blender or food processor with peach liqueur and 4 tablespoons of the cooking juices.

To serve, place a basket on each plate, fill each with two scoops icecream, and cover with peach sauce. Decorate with mint leaves.

Summer Menu Three

Fichi Biondi

FIGS WITH GORGONZOLA SAUCE

~

Orata d'Estate

SNAPPER WITH MINT

~

Fruit "Pizza"

~

*J*ust because it's warm, we don't stop eating. And if we're sensible about it, we can cook for minimum effort and maximum pleasure. This summer menu is an example.

Probably the most common warm weather appetiser in Italian restaurants around the world is figs with prosciutto ham, so we thought it was time to try something new. We decided to cook the figs, wrap them in the prosciutto and enrich the effect with a little gorgonzola cheese (from which we got the name "biondi"—blonde). Warning: these are seriously luscious. Resist the temptation to serve more than two figs per person; there's more to come.

Fresh fish is best when treated simply, so we've grilled our snapper with a little mint and garlic inside. The best accompaniment, we think, is steamed slices of zucchini, carrots, and potatoes, in alternating layers on the plate next to the fish.

We saved the visual spectacle for last. Here's another Italian culinary joke—a "pizza" whose base is a slice of the famous celebratory cake called panettone, with a topping made from the freshest fruits of summer. Instead of cheese, we have cream and icecream.

Panettones come in different sizes, and we're suggesting you buy a small one, so that you can slice it across and make a pizza base for each guest. If you buy a large panettone, you can create a "family size" pizza, and slice it up at the table into individual servings. The effect is highly festive, so it's ideal for a midsummer Christmas in the southern hemisphere. In northern climates, it would suit a fourth of July celebration or summer solstice feast.

Fichi Biondi

....

FIGS WITH GORGONZOLA SAUCE

8 thin slices prosciutto

8 fresh figs

¹/₂ tablespoon butter

1¹/₂ cups (12 fl oz/375 ml) cream

6 oz/180 g gorgonzola or mild blue cheese

Preheat oven to 400°F (200°C/Gas 6).

Wrap one slice of prosciutto around the middle of each fig, and secure ends with toothpick. Melt butter, cream, and gorgonzola together in a saucepan over low heat.

Place figs in an oven-proof dish, pour cream sauce over, and cover dish with foil. Bake for 7 minutes. Remove foil, and bake for 1 minute.

Place two figs on each serving plate, and pour sauce over them.

Orata d'Estate

SNAPPER WITH MINT

4 whole snapper, about 10 oz/315 g each, cleaned

4 cloves garlic, minced

8 mint leaves

7 teaspoons chopped parsley

salt and freshly ground black pepper to taste

5 tablespoons plain (all-purpose) flour

11 tablespoons olive oil

6 tablespoons lemon juice

Inside the belly of each snapper place 1 minced garlic clove, 2 mint leaves, 1 teaspoon parsley, and salt and pepper. Dust each fish with flour. Place fish in a heavy frying pan or on a barbecue, charcoal grill, or hotplate over medium heat, and baste each with 1 tablespoon oil. Cook for 15 minutes if frying, or 10 minutes if using any of the other methods. Turn and cook for another 10 or 15 minutes, basting with another tablespoon of oil for each fish.

Mix 3 tablespoons oil, lemon juice, salt to taste, and 3 teaspoons parsley. Transfer cooked fish onto serving plates and drizzle this sauce over them. Accompany with steamed vegetables.

Fruit "Pizza"

1 panettone or any sponge cake (see recipe on page 13),
   about 4 inches/10 cm in diameter

4 oz/125 g blueberries

4 oz/125 g boysenberries

12 gooseberries

8 strawberries, hulled and halved

1 kiwifruit, peeled and sliced

3 tablespoons maraschino or cherry liqueur

2 teaspoons icing (powdered) sugar

10 oz/315 g raspberries

8 scoops vanilla icecream

3 tablespoons single (light) cream

Slice across the panettone about ¹/₂ inch/1 cm up from the bottom, then cut three more slices about the same thickness, so you have four disks of cake to form the base of your pizzas.

Mix together all fruit, except raspberries. Stir in 1 tablespoon maraschino and 1 teaspoon icing sugar, and let stand for 30 minutes.

Puree raspberries in a blender or food processor with remaining sugar and remaining maraschino. Strain to remove seeds.

Place sponge bases on four individual serving plates and place 2 scoops icecream in the middle of each. Scatter fruit mixture over bases. With a spoon, splash raspberry puree over the pizzas and around the plates. Do the same with cream. Serve immediately.

Summer Menu Four

SERVES 4

Carpaccio Salmonato

~

Angel Hair Pasta with Sage

~

Zuppa di Pesce

FISH SOUP

~

Cherry Cake

~

*T*his menu and the next are for lovers of seafood, which we think is best consumed in warm weather. This one begins with carpaccio salmonato, a name with an odd history. Carpaccio was a 15th century Venetian painter who painted in dark reds, so his name was applied to a dish that contains slices of raw beef marinated in oil and lemon (our version of that appears in Autumn Menu Six). When modern Italian chefs, influenced by the Japanese, started experimenting with raw fish, they adopted the name carpaccio to mean "uncooked" and applied the term to the fish dishes as well, even if their colouring looked nothing like Carpaccio's paintings. Our fine slices of salmon become pale pink after they are marinated, but we're sure the painter would have loved them.

Capelli d'angelo ("angel hair") is the name Italians give to a pasta so thin it needs no more than two minutes cooking. The best form of angel hair pasta is Cipriani. If you can't find Cipriani or any other form of angel hair, just go for the thinnest version of spaghetti available. Because it tastes so fine, this pasta needs no more than sage and butter to bring out its best.

The angel hair forms a delicate bridge to our hearty main course, a fish stew which the Italians modestly call a soup. Because it's from the Mediterranean, it has a lot in common with the French bouillabaise, but we think it's more interesting. You'll need many slices of toasted crusty bread because your guests will insist on soaking up every drop. A basic mignonette lettuce salad with a little olive oil and lemon juice is the only accompaniment it will need.

And while the season's cherries last, let's make a luscious yet light cake that is best eaten hot.

Carpaccio Salmonato

Angel Hair Pasta
with Sage

1 slab fresh salmon, about 8 inches/20 cm long
1 clove garlic, finely minced
6 tablespoons extra virgin olive oil
12 tablespoons lemon juice
1/2 bunch fresh tarragon, finely chopped
salt to taste
freshly ground black pepper to taste

Wrap salmon in plastic wrap, and freeze for about 3 hours. Add garlic to olive oil, and let mixture stand for 3 hours.

Remove salmon from freezer and unwrap. With a very sharp knife, cut horizontally, making slices as thin as possible. Lay slices on four serving plates, without them overlapping. Pour 3 tablespoons lemon juice over each plate. After about 4 minutes the salmon will become a pale pink. Pour off excess lemon juice, and sprinkle with tarragon and a little salt.

The garlic will have sunk to the bottom of the olive oil. Pour 1/2 tablespoon from top of olive oil mixture over each plate of salmon, being careful not to include garlic pieces. Grind pepper over each before serving.

∽

8 oz/250 g angel hair pasta (see page 66)
8 tablespoons butter
4 teaspoons chopped fresh sage
6 tablespoons grated parmesan cheese
salt to taste

Add pasta to boiling water in a large saucepan, and cook for 1½ minutes. Drain and set aside.

In a frying pan, melt butter over low heat. Add sage and then pasta. Stir, then add parmesan and salt. Mix well, and serve.

∽

Zuppa di Pesce

FISH SOUP

1 lb/500 g small calamari (squid), cleaned and ink sacs
    removed

8 tablespoons olive oil

5 whole cloves garlic

8 baby octopus, cleaned and ink sacs removed

5 cups (1.25 l) dry white wine

11 egg (plum) tomatoes, chopped

2 small sand (blue swimmer) crabs, halved

4 rock cod, about 9 oz/280 g each

8 mussels in their shells, scrubbed and stalks removed

8 small clams (vongole), in their shells

8 green king prawns (jumbo shrimp), beheaded but shell
    remaining

2 small red chillies (optional)

salt to taste

1 bunch parsley, chopped

Cut calamari in rings.

Place 2 tablespoons oil and 2 whole cloves garlic in a very large saucepan over medium heat and fry until garlic is golden, about 1 minute. Add octopus and calamari, and stir for 2 minutes. Add 1 cup wine, and cook on high heat for 2 minutes. Add 3 chopped tomatoes, then simmer on low heat for 30 minutes. Add water if sauce begins to dry out.

Preheat oven to 350°F (180°C/Gas 4).

Place remaining oil and garlic in a large baking pan, and fry on stove over medium high heat until garlic is golden, about 1 minute. Add crabs and fry for 3 minutes. Add cod and seal both sides. Add 3 cups wine and 8 tomatoes. Bake in oven for 10 minutes.

Remove from oven and add mussels, clams, and prawns, plus calamari and octopus in their sauce. Add chillies. Cook for 15 minutes over medium heat on stove, adding some of the remaining wine if it begins to dry out. Discard any mussels and clams that do not open. Add salt to taste. Transfer to individual serving bowls and sprinkle with parsley. Serve with crusty bread.

Cherry Cake

3 eggs

8 oz/250 g sugar

12 oz/375 g self-raising flour

7 oz/200 g plain yogurt

4 oz/125 g butter

3 tablespoons olive oil

grated rind of 2 lemons

2 11 fl oz/350 ml cans pitted cherries, drained

icing (powdered) sugar to garnish

single (light) cream to serve

Preheat oven to 425°F (220°C/Gas 7).

Beat eggs and sugar together well. Add flour, yogurt, butter, oil, and lemon rind, one at a time. Mix well.

Grease a 12 inch/28 cm diameter, 3 inch/8 cm deep springform cake pan. Add half the mixture, then push half the cherries into the mixture. Add remaining mixture, then push in remaining cherries.

Bake for 30–40 minutes until a skewer inserted in the middle comes out clean. Sprinkle with icing sugar, and serve hot with cream.

Summer Menu Five

SERVES 4

Rollata di Peperoni

ROLLED CAPSICUM WITH GOAT'S CHEESE

~

Roast Salmon with Asparagus

~

Torta di Fichi

FIG AND MASCARPONE CAKE

~

We did promise to keep the summer menus simple, and we have to admit the first course here involves a bit of work, but the effect is so spectacular we refuse to apologise. It's a great leap forward on the classic Italian roast capsicum. Searing the outside (either in the oven or on top of a gas jet as suggested in Summer Menu One) and then stripping off the skin is just the beginning. Then you roll it around eggplant and goat cheese, top it with pesto sauce and serve it with a cool flourish. When you're shopping, try to choose long capsicums with fairly thin flesh, so they'll roll up easily.

The main course is more straightforward, depending on an inspired combination of ingredients rather than any manual rolling skills. The Italians say "faster than you can cook asparagus" to describe a short space of time, and we would suggest you apply the same caution when cooking both elements in this delicious main course. Salmon is one of those rare fish which is best left pink in the middle (tuna is another). If you need an accompaniment, steamed baby potatoes are ideal.

We go cool again for the dessert, a "cake" that is not cooked. It depends for its impact on very fresh figs, just ripened to a light green by the sun and still pink and moist inside, together with the special whipped mascarpone which we explained at the beginning of the book (see recipe on page 13).

∞

Rollata di Peperoni

ROLLED CAPSICUM WITH GOAT'S CHEESE

4 red capsicums (bell peppers)

salt to taste

10 basil leaves, chopped

1 large eggplant (aubergine), peeled

about 2 tablespoons plain (all-purpose) flour

6 cups (1.5 l) vegetable oil

10 oz/300 g goat's cheese (see glossary)

¹/₂ bunch parsley, chopped

4 teaspoons pesto sauce (see recipe on page 17)

1 tablespoon balsamic vinegar (see glossary)

3 tablespoons olive oil

24 sprigs arugola (rocket) (see glossary)

16 black olives

Preheat oven to 400°F (200°C/Gas 6).

Roast whole capsicums in top part of oven until skin goes wrinkly and starts to lift, about 20 minutes. Remove from oven and allow to cool, then pull off skin, slice around top and bottom, and remove stalk and seeds. Slit capsicums down one side and unroll. (Don't put them under water at any stage.) Lay flat, and sprinkle with salt and basil.

Slice eggplant lengthwise into eight pieces about ¹/₂ inch/1 cm thick. Dust with flour. Heat vegetable oil in frying pan and fry eggplant over high heat for about 3 minutes each side until golden brown. Allow to cool.

Divide goat's cheese into four, and roll each piece into a slim sausage shape, about 1¹/₂ inches/3.5 cm long, with your fingers. Coat with chopped parsley.

To make each roll, lay two strips eggplant end to end down the middle of a capsicum strip (trim to fit, if necessary). Place goat's cheese across the middle of eggplant. Fold capsicum and eggplant over and roll around goat's cheese. Repeat with the other three capsicums, and place each roll on a plate. Spoon 1 teaspoon pesto sauce on top of each roll.

Mix balsamic vinegar and oil in a bowl. Add arugola and olives, and toss gently. Then decorate each plate with six sprigs arugola and four olives.

Roast Salmon with Asparagus

24 fresh asparagus spears

4 tablespoons olive oil

1 clove garlic, minced

4 fillets fresh salmon, about 9 oz/280 g each

1¹/₂ cups (12 fl oz/375 ml) dry white wine

3 tablespoons light meat stock (commercial, or see recipe on page 12)

2 teaspoons black olive paste (commercial)

2 tomatoes, diced

Preheat oven to 350°F (180°C/Gas 4).

Add asparagus to a saucepan of boiling water and boil for 2 minutes, drain, and plunge into cold water for 1 minute. Drain again and set aside.

Place oil and garlic in a baking dish and fry on stove over medium heat until garlic is golden, about 30 seconds. Add salmon, and toss to brown the surface. Add wine.

Bake in oven for 3 minutes, then transfer baking dish to high heat on stove. Add stock, asparagus, and olive paste, and shake pan to mix. Cook for 1 minute.

Place salmon fillets on four plates with asparagus spears on top.

Add tomatoes to the sauce in baking dish. Simmer for 2 minutes to reduce. Pour over salmon.

Torta di Fichi

FIG AND MASCARPONE CAKE

36 savoiardi biscuits (see glossary) or sponge fingers

2 cups (16 fl oz/500 ml) strong black coffee

6 tablespoons coffee liqueur (eg Kahlua or Tia Maria)

3 cups (24 fl oz/750 ml) whipped mascarpone
   (see recipe on page 13)

10 large or 14 small fresh figs, peeled

Dip half of each biscuit in coffee. Lay them to cover bottom of a 12 x 8 inch/30 x 20 cm, 2 inch/5 cm deep dish. Brush them generously with coffee liqueur. Cover with mascarpone to about ¼ inch/5 mm depth.

Cut figs into ½ inch/1 cm thick slices, and layer half on top of mascarpone. Cover again with mascarpone. Repeat with a layer of biscuits, mascarpone, and figs. Cover with plastic wrap, and refrigerate for 3 hours before serving.

Summer Menu Six

SERVES 4

A PICNIC LUNCH

·····················

Frittata di Maccheroni
& Marinated Zucchini
& Insalata Caprese

PASTA AND EGG PIE & MARINATED ZUCCHINI &
TOMATO AND MOZZARELLA SALAD

≈

Pane Rustico

CHEESE BREAD

≈

Pollo alla Diavola

PEPPERED CHICKEN

≈

Fresh Fruit
& Parmesan Cheese

≈

B efore the summer fades, we're off on a picnic, so this menu is designed to be transportable. In fact, you can make everything the day before, to allow a sleep-in on picnic day. Our antipasto —always better eaten cold—involves a traditional Italian method of using up leftover noodles, and includes strongly spiced zucchini, and a tomato salad that is named after the isle of Capri, although Naples often claims credit.

The next element requires you to make your own bread, a process that is always satisfying. This bread has ham and cheese already built in, and if you don't devour it all on the day, it will stay fresh for another week. Then there's the chicken "alla diavola", and you'll see that a brick forms an essential part of the cooking process. If there's no brick ready to hand, put a frying pan on top of the chicken, and a saucepan full of water in the frying pan. This will flatten the chicken so it cooks evenly. Remember, too, that you should grind pepper over it until your grinding arm can stand no more. In this case there's no such thing as too much pepper. We like to say that this dish is named "diavola" (devil) because the chicken goes through hell and tastes like heaven. By the way, you don't need to take the brick to the picnic.

And finally, an assortment of fruit served with the king of cheeses— parmesan. You'll be amazed at how a slice of parmesan boosts the flavour of any fruit. Don't forget to take a sharp knife with you, and a bottle of olive oil—it'll glide helpfully over any of the dishes we've suggested. And as you'll have gathered, this picnic can be just as much fun consumed at your own dining room table.

∞

Frittata di Maccheroni

....

PASTA AND EGG PIE

Marinated Zucchini

....

6 eggs

4 tablespoons grated parmesan cheese

1 lb/500 g pasta (eg fettuccine), cooked

2 oz/60 g ham or bacon, diced

3 egg (plum) tomatoes, diced

4 basil leaves, chopped

oil or butter

salt and freshly ground black pepper to taste

Preheat oven to 325°F (170°C/Gas 3).

Beat eggs well, and mix in parmesan. Add pasta and mix. Add ham, tomato, basil, salt and pepper and mix thoroughly.

Coat a heavy frying pan (with oven-proof handle) or a round baking dish with oil or butter over low heat on stove. Pour in mixture.

Bake in oven for 10 minutes. Turn mixture upside down into a second frying pan or baking dish and bake again for 10 minutes. Can be served hot or cold.

∾

4 zucchini (courgettes)

4 tablespoons olive oil

3 tablespoons light white wine vinegar

3 cloves garlic, minced

¹/₂ bunch mint, roughly chopped

Slice zucchini into thin rings, and lay them out on a dry cloth to dry, preferably in the sun, for about 1 hour.

Heat oil in frying pan over high heat and fry zucchini until golden, about 3 minutes. Drain on paper towels.

Place zucchini in a bowl and pour vinegar over. After about 2 minutes, spread zucchini out on a plate, and sprinkle garlic then mint over. Leave for at least 1 hour. Serve at room temperature.

∾

Insalata Caprese

····················

TOMATO AND MOZZARELLA SALAD

2 ripe tomatoes, sliced thinly

1 mozzarella ball, about 1 oz/30 g, sliced thinly

6 basil leaves, finely chopped

6 tablespoons olive oil

freshly ground black pepper to taste

Interleave tomato and cheese slices on a plate. If you wish to be decorative, you can form them into a circle, or make two rows side by side. Sprinkle generously with basil, and pour oil over them. Grind pepper over the top and serve.

∾

Pane Rustico

····················

CHEESE BREAD

4 cups (1 lb/500 g) plain (all-purpose) flour

3 eggs, lightly beaten

2 tablespoons softened butter

pinch salt

2 tablespoons sugar

1 oz/30 g fresh yeast

1 cup (8 fl oz/250 ml) milk, room temperature

3¹/₂ oz/100 g provolone (see glossary) or other strong-tasting cheese, grated

3¹/₂ oz/100 g emmenthal or other mild Swiss cheese, grated

3¹/₂ oz/100 g prosciutto (see glossary), bacon or ham, cubed

2 tablespoons olive oil

On a smooth working surface (marble is ideal), place flour in a mound. Form a hole in the middle, and add eggs, butter, salt, sugar, and yeast. Mix with your hands, slowly adding milk. Knead until a soft dough is formed.

Scatter cheeses and prosciutto through dough and knead again. Shape into a long loaf. Let rest 2 hours.

Preheat oven to 400°F (200°C/Gas 6).

Butter a round 14 inch/35 cm diameter, 3 inch/7 cm deep brioche or a cake pan with a cup turned down in the middle. Place dough inside. Bake for 40 minutes or until a skewer inserted in the middle comes out clean.

∾

Pollo alla Diavola

PEPPERED CHICKEN

1 large chicken
2 cups (15 fl oz/500 ml) dry white wine
3 tablespoons olive oil
3 bay leaves
pinch salt
freshly ground black pepper
2 clean house bricks or other weights
juice of 2 lemons

Cut chicken in half lengthwise, and marinate overnight in wine, oil, bay leaves, and salt.

Open up, then flatten chicken halves. Place chicken, with the inside down, in a large frying pan on high heat (or on the hotplate of a barbecue). Grind *lots* of black pepper over chicken (don't be timid). Place a brick or other weight on top of each half. Turn chicken over after 20 minutes, grind on more pepper, and cook under the weights for a further 20 minutes.

Serve hot or cold with lemon juice squeezed over.

∾

Fresh Fruit and Parmesan Cheese

assorted fruit in season (eg melons, cherries, mangoes, kiwifruit, bananas, pears)
10 oz/315 g piece parmesan cheese
extra virgin olive oil

When ready to eat, peel, slice, and mix fruit to your taste. Slice the parmesan, and sandwich pieces of fruit between slices of cheese. Also try dipping cheese into olive oil.

Autumn Menu One

SERVES 4

Orecchiette Pasta with Broccoli

≈

Grilled Quails with Eggplant Puree

≈

Dolce dell'Angelo

SWEET PASTA PIE

≈

As the golden leaves start to fall, eager eaters such as us face a new range of exciting possibilities, not just in the different produce which reaches its peak in autumn but also in the opportunity offered by the cooler weather to indulge in meals that are a little richer than would be comfortable in summer. We begin with "orecchiette" pasta—literally translated as "little ears"—served with a substantial broccoli sauce. We suggest you spice it up with a little chilli, as would be done in Puglia, the southern region of Italy where the dish originated.

Our main course—quails marinated for 24 hours then barbecued and served with a nourishing eggplant puree—shows the Middle Eastern influence that is significant in Italy's south, a legacy of Arab invasions over the centuries. We think it works best if you use high heat to make the quails' skin crunchy, creating a texture contrast with the smooth puree. You could serve it with braised leeks: just slice the leeks lengthwise, wash them and fry them in olive oil for about 5 minutes.

Our dessert derives from Jewish-Italian cooking—a mixture of candied fruits, orange blossom water (a heady fragrance you might want to try as a perfume), and pasta (which could be your leftovers from the day before). Don't be greedy with this one; keep the layer of pasta in the baking dish fairly thin (less than an inch thick) so that it cooks evenly. And there's your feast to welcome the cool change.

∾

Orecchiette Pasta with Broccoli

8 oz/250 g orecchiette pasta (see glossary)

3 oz/90 g broccoli, heads only

4 tablespoons olive oil

1 clove garlic, finely chopped

1 small dried chilli (optional)

8 basil leaves, chopped

4 tablespoons grated pecorino
   or parmesan cheese

Boil pasta, about 7 minutes. Drain.

Boil broccoli until tender, about 5 minutes.

Place oil, garlic, and chilli in frying pan over medium high heat and fry for 1 minute. Add broccoli and stir over medium heat for 4 minutes. Add pasta and basil, and mix well.

Place into four serving bowls, and sprinkle with grated cheese.

Grilled Quails with Eggplant Puree

8 quails, split and cleaned

1 24 fl oz/750 ml bottle dry white wine

8 bay leaves

5 cloves garlic

pinch salt

2 tablespoons vegetable oil

3 medium eggplants (aubergines)

2 tablespoons chopped parsley

salt and freshly ground black pepper to taste

1 cup (8 fl oz/250 ml) meat stock (commercial,
    or see recipe on page 12), warmed

Marinate quails for 24 hours in a mixture of wine, bay leaves, 4 cloves garlic (halved), and salt. Be sure quails are covered by marinade.

Preheat oven to 400°F (200°C/Gas 6).

Rub oil on skin of eggplants, place on baking sheet and bake for 20 minutes. Remove from oven, allow to cool, and peel off skin. Puree eggplants in blender with 1 small clove garlic (crushed) and parsley. Season with salt and pepper.

Place quails on charcoal grill, barbecue, or hotplate, or in a heavy frying pan, belly side down. Cook for 12 minutes on each side.

Heat eggplant puree in a frying pan over low heat, and place a dollop in the middle of each serving plate. Put two quails on each plate, and spoon 3 tablespoons warmed meat stock on top.

Accompany with braised leeks.

Dolce dell'Angelo

·······································

SWEET PASTA PIE

12 oz/375 g angel hair pasta

5 eggs, beaten

8 tablespoons sugar

¹/₂ teaspoon ground cinnamon

¹/₂ teaspoon vanilla powder or extract

3 tablespoons orange blossom water (see glossary) or
   orange liqueur

2 oz/60 g orange peel, diced

2 oz/60 g candied fruit (eg "cedro" lemon) (see glossary)

2 oz/60 g unsweetened cooking chocolate or dark semi-sweet
   chocolate, diced

butter for greasing

icing (powdered) sugar for sprinkling

whipped cream to serve

Preheat oven to 350°F (180°C/Gas 4).

Boil pasta for 1 minute, then drain.

Mix eggs with sugar, cinnamon, vanilla, and orange blossom water. Add pasta and mix. Add orange peel, candied fruit, and chocolate. Mix well.

Butter a large round cake pan or oven-proof frying pan, preferably nonstick. Pour in mixture. Bake for 7 minutes. Turn pie upside down into another pan and bake for a further 5 minutes. Remove and sprinkle with sugar.

Serve hot or cold with cream.

ം

Autumn Menu Two

SERVES 4

Antipasto of Mushroom Frittata & Stuffed Zucchini & Spicy Cauliflower

∾

Truffled Eggs

∾

Involtini di Salmone

SALMON ROLLS

∾

Torta di Mandorle

ALMOND CAKE

∾

We begin this banquet with a triple-header antipasto. It contains mouthfuls of zucchini that are easy to make and easier to eat with the fingers; steamed cauliflower, a vegetable best eaten in autumn and here boosted with white wine and a touch of chilli; and a frittata (a kind of omelette) made with mushrooms. The mushrooms offer a chance to be adventurous—white button mushrooms are fine, but in autumn a wide range of strangely shaped and strongly-flavoured fungi should be available, all of which can be chopped up and thrown in to enhance this dish.

Next comes one of the supreme smell and taste experiences the world can offer—white truffles. We're assuming that you're not in a position to lay your hands on fresh white truffles to grate over your pasta, but your local gourmet supplier might stock the next best thing: eggs that have been flavoured with truffle. This is achieved by leaving the eggs and a fresh truffle in a sealed container for several days so that the aroma is absorbed through the eggshell. It's worth a search to find these, but if that fails, you'll have less trouble finding olive oil that has been flavoured with truffles, and that is what we use in our recipe. For a lighter version, eliminate the butter and cream, and toss the cooked pasta in truffled oil in the frying pan.

After that, we're suggesting you use that versatile fish, salmon, to make "involtini", a dish normally made with veal fillets. Thin potato chips make a crunchy accompaniment: deep fry them in the lightest olive oil you can find over medium to high heat for about 7 minutes.

Our banquet concludes with a liqueur-soaked almond cake from the area around Venice. Italians are passionate about almond trees. In spring, their hearts lift as the brilliant pink and white flowers blossom, and they wait through the summer as the almonds ripen to perfection. Now we are ready for them.

Mushroom Frittata

4 egg (plum) tomatoes, halved

about 3 tablespoons olive oil

12 eggs, beaten

4 tablespoons grated parmesan cheese

6 tablespoons single (light) cream

salt and freshly ground black pepper to taste

6 oz/150 g button mushrooms (champignons)
   or other mushrooms, sliced

1/2 clove garlic, minced

4 basil leaves, chopped

Preheat oven to 350°F (180°C/Gas 4). Bake tomatoes in baking dish with 1 tablespoon oil for 10 minutes. Chop roughly.

Oil a large but shallow, round, oven-proof pan. Mix parmesan, cream, salt, and pepper into eggs. Pour half the egg mixture into prepared pan and bake for 5 minutes.

Meanwhile, place 2 tablespoons oil, mushrooms, and garlic in a frying pan over high heat and fry for 4 minutes. Drain the oil.

Remove pan from oven, top the egg mixture with chopped tomatoes and mushrooms, sprinkle on basil, and cover with remaining egg mixture. Bake for another 12 minutes or until egg has set. Remove from oven and allow to rest for 3 minutes.

Turn out onto a plate, and serve hot or cold.

Stuffed Zucchini

4 zucchini (courgettes), preferably long and slim

6 cups (1.5 l) chicken stock (water with commercial chicken stock cubes will do)

3 tablespoons olive oil

1/2 clove garlic, minced

1/2 red capsicum (bell pepper), chopped finely

3 tablespoons ricotta cheese

6 basil leaves, chopped

salt and freshly ground black pepper to taste

Cut zucchini into cylinders about 2 inches/5 cm long, and scoop out the inside of each cylinder to about three-quarters of its depth. Bring stock to a boil in a large saucepan. Add zucchini pieces and boil for 8 minutes, remove from stock, and allow to cool.

Place oil and garlic in a frying pan over medium high heat and fry until garlic is golden, about 30 seconds. Add capsicum and cook for 2 minutes. Add ricotta, basil, salt and pepper, and cook for another 2 minutes. Fill each zucchini piece with this mixture, and serve at room temperature.

∽

Spicy Cauliflower

1 medium cauliflower, leaves and stalk removed

3 tablespoons olive oil

2 whole cloves garlic

3 whole baby red chillies (optional)

3/4 cup (6 fl oz/180 ml) dry white wine

3 egg (plum) tomatoes, chopped

2 tablespoons chopped parsley

Chop cauliflower into pieces, wash, and drain.

Place oil and garlic in frying pan over medium high heat and fry until garlic is golden, about 1 minute. Add chillies and cauliflower, toss, and fry for 1 minute. Add 1/2 cup wine. Cover and cook for 5 minutes over medium heat.

Add tomatoes and remaining white wine. Cover and cook for another 10 minutes. Stir in parsley. Serve either warm or at room temperature.

∽

Truffled Eggs

9 oz/280 g dry or fresh fettuccine

1 tablespoon butter

1 cup (8 fl oz/250 ml) light (single) cream

4 tablespoons grated parmesan cheese

4 tablespoons truffled olive oil (see page 90)

4 eggs

extra parmesan cheese for serving

Boil fettuccine for about 6 minutes if dry or 4 minutes if fresh. Drain.

Add butter and cream to a frying pan and simmer for 3 minutes over medium heat to reduce the mixture. Add pasta and toss, then add parmesan and stir.

Coat a frying pan generously with truffled olive oil, and fry eggs until whites are firm, but yolks are still runny.

Divide pasta into four bowls and sit an egg on top of each. Toss egg into pasta in front of each diner. Add more parmesan if desired.

Involtini di Salmone

·····································

SALMON ROLLS

4 bunches English spinach, stems removed

1 tablespoon butter

2 cloves garlic, chopped

8 slices fresh salmon, about ¹/₄ inch/5 mm thick

5 tablespoons olive oil

6 green spring onions, scallions, or shallots, sliced finely

1 cup (8 fl oz/250 ml) dry white wine

12 egg (plum) tomatoes, chopped

4 basil leaves, finely chopped

Boil spinach for 5 minutes, drain, and chop. Melt butter in a frying pan over low heat, add garlic, then stir in spinach. Divide mixture into eight parts.

Lay salmon slices flat, and place a dollop of spinach mixture in the middle of each. Roll slices up, and secure each one with a toothpick.

Place oil and onions in frying pan over medium high heat and fry until onions are soft, about 1 minute. Add rolled salmon, and toss over high heat to seal the surface. Add wine, and simmer until it evaporates. Add tomatoes, and simmer for 8 minutes.

Remove toothpicks. Serve sprinkled with basil.

Torta di Mandorle

······························

ALMOND CAKE

CAKE:

12 eggs, separated

5 tablespoons sugar

pinch salt

14 oz/400 g ground almonds

2 tablespoons self-raising flour

grated rind of 1 lemon

1¹/2 tablespoons amaretto or other sweet almond liqueur

butter

plain (all-purpose) flour

TOPPING AND FILLING:

3¹/2 oz/100 g unsalted butter, softened

3¹/2 oz/100 g caster (superfine) sugar

1 egg, beaten

¹/4 teaspoon vanilla powder or extract

a little amaretto or other sweet almond liqueur

sliced almonds for decoration

Preheat oven to 425°F (220°C/Gas 7).

Mix yolks with sugar until creamy. Beat whites until stiff (a pinch of salt makes this easier). Fold in yolk mixture. Slowly fold in almonds and flour. Gently mix in grated rind and liqueur.

Butter a 12 inch/28 cm diameter, 4 inch/8 cm deep cake pan, and dust with flour. Pour in mixture, and bake for 30 minutes or until a skewer inserted in the middle comes out clean.

To make topping and filling, beat butter with caster sugar. Add egg and vanilla. Work with a wooden spoon until smooth and translucent.

Cut cake in half. Wet the middle with liqueur. Fill with ¹/4 inch/5 mm thickness of butter mixture. Replace top half of cake, and cover top and sides with remaining butter mixture. Decorate with sliced almonds.

∞

Autumn Menu Three

SERVES 4

Penne with Saffron

~

Octopus Casserole

~

Frolla Napoli

FRUIT PASTRY

~

Saffron has been described as the most pungent and the most expensive spice in the world. It grew wild in ancient Italy (under the name crocus) and the Romans loved it, but its modern name came from the Arabs. Our recipe spreads the saffron with cream, and accentuates the dish with garlic and herbs, but if you want to really focus on the crocus, you can leave out the garlic and rosemary. We've suggested saffron threads, but if you can't find them, saffron powder will give you the head-clearing odour with less visual drama.

Octopus casserole is a favourite of the fisherfolk of southern Italy, who can often be seen hurling their octopus against rocks to tenderise them before they go into the pot. If you buy small octopus, you probably won't need to bash them at all, although the exercise is useful for building an appetite. We haven't included chilli in the recipe, but feel free to sizzle a couple of whole small chillis with the garlic for a sauce with more kick. We like dipping lots of toasted slices of dense Italian bread into the sauce, and we suggest that the best accompaniment is a simple salad of sharp leaves such as arugola or radicchio.

The dessert is part of the staple diet of Naples, a candied fruit pastry that shows its 18th century origins by the inclusion of sugar and dripping in quantities that might alarm modern health fanatics. You have three good reasons to indulge (with whipped cream)—the earlier components of the meal were light and spicy in anticipation of this rich conclusion; late autumn weather requires good internal insulation; and it's important for you to experience a slice of Italy's cultural history in its original form.

Penne with Saffron

9 oz/280 g penne

3 tablespoons butter

2 teaspoons chopped garlic

about 1 cup (8 fl oz/250 ml) single (light) cream

4 teaspoons chopped fresh sage

1/2 teaspoon saffron strands

4 teaspoons chopped fresh rosemary

salt to taste

4 tablespoons grated parmesan cheese

5 basil leaves, chopped

freshly ground black pepper

Boil penne, about 7 minutes.

Meanwhile, melt butter in frying pan over medium low heat and fry garlic until golden, about 30 seconds. Stir in cream, sage, saffron, and rosemary, and bring to boil. Reduce heat to medium. Sprinkle with salt.

Drain penne and add to the frying pan, stirring in parmesan immediately afterwards. If mixture seems a bit dry, add more cream. Divide into four bowls, and sprinkle with basil and pepper.

∞

99

Octopus Casserole

5 tablespoons olive oil

3 cloves garlic, whole

24 baby octopus, cleaned and ink sacs removed

20 black olives, pitted

3 tablespoons capers, soaked in water for 30 minutes
    and drained

about 2 cups (16 fl oz/500 ml) dry white wine

2¼ lb/1.125 kg fresh or canned tomatoes, pureed

2 tablespoons chopped fresh basil

Place oil and garlic in a casserole dish or deep saucepan over medium heat and fry until garlic is golden, about 1 minute. Add octopus and cook for 1 minute. Add olives, capers, and wine, and cook for 3 minutes. Add tomato puree, reduce heat to medium, and cook for 30 minutes. If sauce dries out, add more wine. Sprinkle with basil.

Accompany with toasted bread and a green leaf salad.

Frolla Napoli

PASTRY:

1 lb/500 g plain (all-purpose) flour

pinch salt

7 oz/220 g sugar

about 10 tablespoons water

6 oz/180 g dripping

FILLING:

2 cups (16 fl oz/500 ml) water

5 oz/140 g semolina

¹/₂ teaspoon salt

4 oz/120 g ricotta cheese

4¹/₂ oz/130 g sugar

1 egg

2 oz/50 g candied fruit, chopped

¹/₄ teaspoon vanilla powder or extract

2 tablespoons orange blossom water (see glossary)

plain (all-purpose) flour for dusting

1 egg yolk, beaten

butter for greasing

icing (powdered) sugar for sprinkling

TO MAKE THE PASTRY: make a mound of the flour with a well in the middle. Add salt then sugar, water, and dripping in stages, mixing slowly into flour using your fingers, until all flour is absorbed. Continue kneading until dough is elastic. Set aside for 1 hour.

Place 2 cups water in saucepan over medium heat. Add semolina and salt, and stir for 10 minutes. Set aside to cool.

Push ricotta through a sieve, and beat in sugar and egg. Add candied fruit and vanilla. Stir in orange blossom water and cooled semolina.

Preheat oven to 400°F (200°C/Gas 6).

Sprinkle work surface with flour. Roll dough out thinly. Cut into circles about 4 inches/10 cm in diameter. Place 2 tablespoons of filling in the middle of half the circles. Cover each one with another circle. Press edges with a fork to seal. Brush tops with egg yolk.

Place in a buttered baking dish and bake until golden, about 15–20 minutes.

Remove from oven, and sprinkle with icing sugar.

Autumn Menu Four

SERVES 4

Torta di Polenta

POLENTA, PUMPKIN, AND SPINACH CAKE

∾

Pollo alla Marsala

CHICKEN LEGS WITH PORCINI MUSHROOMS
AND MARSALA

∾

Coppa d'Autunno

FRUIT SUNDAE

∾

ere's a menu that features two of the most ancient delicacies of northern Italy—polenta and porcini, and one of the great wines of southern Italy—marsala. It begins with what we consider the most visually striking dish in this book, a "cake" made with alternating layers of yellow polenta, green spinach, crimson beetroot, and orange pumpkin.

Polenta is corn meal which turns into a savoury porridge, and a version of it, made with wheat, was carried in the pouches of the Roman legionnaries on their journeys of conquest across Europe. It was history's first "instant dinner"—just add water. We doubt if those war-weary warriors went to the trouble of turning their polenta into a multicoloured cake, but that is their loss. It is likely that they'd have carried dried porcini mushrooms in their pouches too, if they had time to pick them on their way through the forests of northern Italy.

The word "porcini" has the same origin as the word for pork. Its name arose from the alleged fondness of pigs for these large and powerfully-flavoured fungi. Here we're combining them with chicken and with marsala, the highly alcoholic, slightly sweet wine made in the south west of Sicily since the 17th century. If you can't find marsala, you could use madeira or tokai fortified wine (but not egg marsala liqueur). It's a rich and rewarding dish served on a bed of rice, and we're suggesting a cold fruit dessert to balance it—a colourful "sundae" boosted by our special whipped mascarpone mixture.

Torta di Polenta

POLENTA, PUMPKIN, AND SPINACH CAKE

8 cups (2 l) water
3 bay leaves
2 teaspoons salt
1 1/2 lb/750 g polenta
5 tablespoons parmesan cheese, grated
5 tablespoons unsalted butter
5 large beet (beetroots), chopped
a pinch of grated fresh ginger
1 teaspoon hot chilli sauce or to taste
1/2 blue pumpkin, peeled and diced
1/2 bunch fresh sage, chopped
3 bunches English spinach

SAUCE:
6 tablespoons gorgonzola or mild blue cheese
1/2 tablespoon butter
3 tablespoons light (single) cream

Bring water, bay leaves, and salt to a boil in a large saucepan. Slowly whisk in polenta powder. Reduce heat, and cook for about 1 hour, whisking regularly, until it forms a thick porridge. Add more hot water if the polenta dries out. Remove bay leaves and mix in 2 tablespoons parmesan and 2 tablespoons butter.

Butter a large cake pan, preferably a nonstick, spring-form pan, 12 inches/28cm in diameter and 4 inches/8 cm deep. Pour in polenta and leave to cool.

Meanwhile, boil beets for 20 minutes. Puree, adding ginger and chilli sauce.

Steam pumpkin for 15 minutes. Puree, then toss it in a frying pan over medium heat with 2 tablespoons melted butter and sage.

Boil spinach for 5 minutes. Puree, then quickly fry in 1 tablespoon butter with 3 tablespoons parmesan over medium heat.

Remove polenta cake from cake pan, and slice it horizontally into three disks, each about 1/2 inch/1 cm thick. Put first layer back in pan, and cover with beet puree. Place another polenta layer on top of this, and cover with pumpkin puree. Put the third polenta layer on top, and cover with spinach puree. Refrigerate for 2 hours to set. Remove 1 hour before serving.

Just before serving, slice cake and place into an oven, preheated to 400°F (200°C/Gas 6), for three minutes. Meanwhile, make sauce by melting cheese, butter, and cream together in a saucepan over low heat.

Pour a puddle of sauce on each serving plate, then place a heated wedge of cake on top of the sauce.

∞

Pollo alla Marsala

······································

CHICKEN LEGS WITH PORCINI MUSHROOMS AND MARSALA

12 chicken drumsticks

8 tablespoons plain (all-purpose) flour

3¹/₂ tablespoons butter

1¹/₂ large or 2 small onions, chopped

2 carrots, peeled and diced

7 oz/220 g button mushrooms (champignons), chopped

3¹/₂ oz/100 g ham, chopped

2 oz/60 g prosciutto (see glossary) or bacon, chopped

2 cups (16 fl oz/500 ml) marsala wine

1 oz/30 g dried porcini mushrooms (see glossary), soaked in lukewarm water for 1 hour

boiled white rice to serve

Preheat oven to 350°F (180°C/Gas 4).

Dust drumsticks with flour. Melt butter in an oven-proof pan on stove, and fry onion and carrot for 3 minutes over high heat. Add button mushrooms, ham, and prosciutto. Add drumsticks, and fry until browned, about 2 minutes. Add marsala.

Squeeze excess water from porcini mushrooms, and add to pan. Cover with foil, and bake in oven for 30 minutes. Check after 15 minutes, and if the sauce is drying out, add ¹/₂ cup (4 fl oz/125 ml) water.

Place three drumsticks on each plate on a bed of rice, and pour sauce over.

Coppa d'Autunno

FRUIT SUNDAE

6 eggs, separated

5 tablespoons sugar

4 cups (32 fl oz/1 l) light (single) cream, beaten

9 oz/280 g strawberries, cubed

1 banana, cubed

1 kiwifruit, cubed

3 tablespoons maraschino or other cherry liqueur

16 tablespoons whipped mascarpone (see recipe on page 13)

2 passionfruit, halved

TO MAKE A SEMIFREDDO: beat egg yolks with sugar until stiff. Beat egg whites until stiff. Fold cream into yolks. Then gently fold egg whites into mixture. Cover and freeze for at least 4 hours.

Meanwhile, soak cubed fruit in liqueur for about 1 hour.

Into each of four sundae glasses, layer 2 scoops semifreddo, followed by a quarter of the fruit, and then 4 tablespoons mascarpone. Spoon pulp from half a passionfruit on top of each.

∼

Autumn Menu Five

SERVES 4

Linguine in Cartoccio

SEAFOOD PASTA PARCEL

∾

Salsicce alla Toscana

SPICY SAUSAGES AND BEANS

∾

Insalata di Montagna

RADICCHIO SALAD WITH BACON AND
GOAT'S CHEESE

∾

Pere al Cioccolato

BAKED PEARS WITH CHOCOLATE SAUCE

∾

A sense of theatre is an important part of being a good host, and this meal begins with a theatrical flourish—you deliver to each guest a small, neatly wrapped paper parcel. Guests open their parcels themselves, and their nostrils are immediately seduced by the fragrant mixture of basil, garlic, wine, and seafood that has been trapped inside. You can use foil instead of baking paper (parchment) in this recipe if you wish, but we think guests find paper more surprising. Just be sure not to use paper that will get soggy. You may notice that in this recipe the linguine noodles are boiled for less time than we usually recommend. That's because the cooking process continues when the pasta is mixed with the seafood sauce and baked in the oven. We want to be sure the pasta emerges from its wrapping paper as "al dente".

The feast continues with a tribute to Tuscany. Italians refer to the people who live around Florence as "mangiafagioli" ("bean-eaters") and here we've mixed small cannellini beans with another Tuscan favourite, spicy sausages. Yes, it's a heavy dish, fit for peasants and hungry kings, so we're suggesting a sharp "mountain" salad of radicchio and goat cheese to balance it. That way your palate and stomach are reconciled before confronting the decadent dessert of pears with a dense syrup and a dark chocolate sauce. Our favourite way of eating this is to serve the pears cold and the sauce warm. We can't advise you on how much cream to add, except to say that there should be enough white to provide a noticeable contrast with the dark brown and the gold.

∞

Linguine in Cartoccio

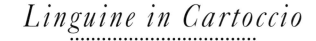

SEAFOOD PASTA PARCEL

5 small calamari (squid), cleaned and ink sacs removed

6 tablespoons olive oil

3 cloves garlic

2 cups (16 fl oz/500 ml) dry white wine

1 small hot red chilli (optional)

20 green prawns (shrimp), peeled

20 mussels in their shells, cleaned and debearded

2 tomatoes, chopped

6 basil leaves, chopped

salt and freshly ground black pepper to taste

9 oz/280 g linguine (see glossary)

Preheat oven to 400°F (200°C/Gas 6).

Separate tentacles from bodies of calamari, and cut bodies into rings. Place 2 tablespoons oil and 1 clove garlic, crushed, in a frying pan over medium heat and fry until garlic is golden, about 30 seconds. Add rings and tentacles, and fry for 2½ minutes. Add 1 cup wine. Simmer for 20 minutes, adding more wine if it starts to dry out. Set aside.

In a large frying pan over medium heat, place chilli and remaining oil and garlic, chopped. Add prawns and mussels, cook until mussel shells open, about 2 minutes. Discard any that do not. Remove mussels from shells, and return mussels to pan. Add calamari with its liquid, and cook for 3 minutes. Add tomatoes, basil, salt and pepper, and cook for another 5 minutes over low heat.

Meanwhile, boil linguine for 5 minutes. Drain, and add to frying pan. Mix thoroughly.

Lay out 4 sheets of baking paper (parchment), and put a quarter of the linguine and sauce into the middle of each sheet. Fold the paper over twice, and fold over the top and ends. Heat on baking tray in oven for 1 minute. Serve wrapped parcels for guests to open.

Salsicce alla Toscana

SPICY SAUSAGES AND BEANS

Insalata di Montagna

RADICCHIO SALAD WITH BACON AND GOAT'S CHEESE

9 oz/280 g cannellini beans (see glossary)
2 tablespoons olive oil
1 clove garlic, minced
2 teaspoons chopped fresh sage
12 Italian sausages or any spicy sausages
9 oz/280 g tomatoes, chopped
salt and freshly ground black pepper to taste

Soak beans overnight in water to cover. Strain, and simmer in fresh water for 30 minutes. Strain and set aside, reserving cooking water.

Heat oil in a frying pan over medium heat, and fry garlic and sage for 30 seconds. Prick sausages with fork, add to pan, and fry for 5 minutes. Add tomatoes and 2 cups bean water. Simmer for 20 minutes, adding more bean water if the mixture begins to dry out. Add beans, and simmer for another 10 minutes. Season with salt and pepper just before serving.

∾

2 radicchio lettuces, leaves only (see glossary)
1 mignonette lettuce, leaves only (see glossary)
salt and pepper to taste
3/4 cup (6 fl oz/180 ml) olive oil
8 tablespoons chopped bacon
4 tablespoons pine nuts
2 oz/60 g mushrooms, chopped
3 1/2 oz/100 g goat's cheese, cubed (see glossary)

Place lettuce leaves in a large bowl, and season with salt and pepper.

Heat oil in a frying pan, and fry bacon, pine nuts, and mushrooms for 2 minutes. Add to bowl with lettuce, and mix well.

Arrange lettuce leaves in a rose pattern on serving plates. Spoon over any bacon, mushrooms, and pine nuts remaining in the bowl. Top with goat's cheese.

∾

Pere al Cioccolato

BAKED PEARS WITH CHOCOLATE SAUCE

6 tablespoons sugar

4 cups (32 fl oz/1 l) sweet white wine

4 brown pears, with stems

$^1/_2$ stick cinnamon or 2 teaspoons ground

3 tablespoons pear liqueur (eg Calvados)

8 oz/250 g unsweetened cooking chocolate

about 2 tablespoons single (light) cream

Preheat oven to 350°F (180°C/Gas 4).

Mix sugar and wine, and pour into a baking dish. Add whole pears and cinnamon. Cover with foil, and bake for 20 minutes. Remove from oven, and set pears aside. Cook the liquid on the stove over high heat until sauce thickens, about 7 minutes. Towards the end, add pear liqueur. Remove cinnamon stick.

Melt chocolate in a saucepan over very low heat. Combine with cream.

Pour pear sauce onto serving plates. Stand a pear on each. Starting at the top, pour about 2 tablespoons of chocolate sauce down each pear.

Autumn Menu Six

SERVES 4

Pumpkin Risotto

~

*Hot Beef Carpaccio
with Polenta*

~

Formaggi e Canditi Misti

CHEESES AND DRIED FRUITS

~

R isotto is such an obsession with northern Italians that they'd like you to believe it's almost impossible to make. Certainly risotto is more than the boiled rice with sauce that some lazy restaurateurs would offer, but it's far from difficult, as long as you're prepared to spend a bit of time. The point is to keep stirring and to add the broth very slowly after letting the rice come close to drying out, repeating the process several times. The result in this case is hearty and luscious, with the pumpkin adding sweetness to the plump rice. The most amusing way to serve this is inside partly hollowed out small pumpkins, so that the guests can lift the lids and discover their risotto—more of that theatre we mentioned in the last menu. If you can't find small pumpkins, bowls will do fine. You might like to sprinkle a few pieces of crunchy fried bacon over the risotto. The northern Italians like to grate truffles over it, and if you can find a truffle, go for it.

Next comes our version of carpaccio, the raw beef dish named after the Venetian painter who loved deep red colours. Actually ours is cooked just a little, but it has to remain very rare so that the meat flavour is strong enough to blend with the vigorous sauce of pepper, worcestershire sauce, and balsamic vinegar. We think it's essential to serve this in the northern Italian fashion with squares of crunchy grilled polenta (see the recipe on page 13), which will soak up the delicious juices. If you feel in need of vegetable accompaniment, we suggest steamed cauliflower and steamed snow peas, drizzled with a little olive oil. The meal ends with deceptive simplicity—a mixture of cheeses and candied and dried fruits. You can make this an experiment in texture and flavour contrasts—test your local suppliers by demanding their best examples of soft, semi-soft and hard cheese. Be sure to take all the cheeses out of the refrigerator at least an hour before the meal.

Pumpkin Risotto

RISOTTO:

4 oz/125 g unsalted butter

1 onion, chopped

9 oz/280 g arborio rice (see glossary)

7 cups (1.75 l) chicken stock, warmed over low heat

³/4 large blue pumpkin, peeled and diced

3 teaspoons chopped fresh sage

10 tablespoons grated parmesan cheese

SAUCE:

¹/4 large blue pumpkin, peeled and diced

1¹/2 oz/50 g butter

1 cup (8 fl oz/250 ml) dry white wine

TO MAKE THE RISOTTO: melt butter in a large frying pan and fry onion until soft, about 3 minutes. Add rice, and stir over low heat for 3 to 4 minutes. Add one ladle of stock, and stir rice constantly with wooden spoon until liquid is absorbed, about 4 minutes. Add another ladle and pumpkin, and stir. Keep adding stock slowly and stirring constantly for 20 minutes, cooking both rice and pumpkin, and adding sage after 15 minutes.

FOR THE SAUCE: melt butter in a frying pan, add pumpkin and wine and cook until pumpkin is soft, about 4 minutes. Puree.

Add parmesan to risotto and stir. Divide risotto between four serving bowls or small, hollowed-out pumpkins, pour sauce over the top, and serve.

Hot Beef Carpaccio with Polenta

4 tablespoons olive oil

1 clove garlic, minced

4 teaspoons Worcestershire sauce

4 teaspoons balsamic vinegar

3 cups (24 fl oz/750 ml) meat stock (commercial, or see recipe on page 12)

2 tablespoons freshly ground black pepper

1¹/₂ lbs/750 g beef fillet, trimmed

1 bunch arugola (rocket) for garnish (see glossary)

grilled polenta (see recipe on page 13)

Place 3 tablespoons of oil and garlic in a frying pan over medium heat, and fry until garlic is golden, about 30 seconds. Pour off excess oil, retaining garlic in the pan. Add Worcestershire sauce, vinegar, and meat stock, and simmer for 5 minutes. Add pepper, and simmer for 1 minute.

Brush a heated frying pan or hotplate with remaining olive oil. Seal fillet over medium heat for 5 minutes on each side. Allow to rest for 2 minutes. Cut into slices about ¹/₂ inch/1 cm thick. Arrange pieces on a large plate, and cover with sauce. Decorate with arugola. Serve with a separate plate of grilled polenta.

Formaggi e Canditi Misti

CHEESES AND DRIED FRUITS

For a light end to a hearty meal, serve about 4 oz/125 g of each of these cheeses: Bel Paese, brie or camembert, provolone or parmesan (see glossary). Accompany these with about 4 oz/ 125 g each of candied fruit, dates, sultanas (golden raisins), and dried apricots.

Winter Menu One

SERVES 4

Zuppa con Polpette

CHICKEN SOUP WITH MEAT BALLS

~

Farfalle con le Mandorle

BUTTERFLY PASTA WITH ALMOND SAUCE

~

Involtini di Spinaci

VEAL ROLLS WITH SPINACH

~

Torta di Mele

APPLE CAKE

~

We look forward eagerly to the chilly winds of winter because they mean more meat, superior soups, and the chance to eat rich creamy sauces with a clear conscience. Here's a menu combining all of those pleasures. Chicken broth forms the base of the first recipe, and while you might use a commercial stock, there's no substitute for the broth you make yourself—quite apart from its value in keeping the kitchen warm for hours. (In this case you'll be left with a very well-cooked piece of poultry and some very soft vegetables. Put them in the refrigerator and when you want a quick snack, fry them with oil and garlic and toss them on pasta.) The broth gets even heartier with the addition of meatballs, potatoes, and silverbeet or spinach.

Next comes a pretty pasta with a magnificent almond and mascarpone sauce that is so rich we've deliberately kept the main course simple—a northern Italian dish of veal rolled around spinach, enhanced with a Mediterranean tomato sauce. We suggest you serve it with mashed potato to soak up the various juices.

The dessert is light and refreshing—the purest essence of apple flavour and a concentrated dose of vitamin C. Although we call it a cake, there's no flour and no eggs, just very finely sliced apples with a touch of ginger for sharpness and pistachio nuts for texture contrast.

∽

Zuppa con Polpette

CHICKEN SOUP WITH MEAT BALLS

3 tablespoons olive oil

1 onion, chopped

1 celery stalk, chopped

2 carrots, chopped

10 peppercorns

1 whole chicken, about 3¹/₂ lb/1.75 kg, cleaned

10 oz/315 g soft bread, crusts removed

1¹/₂ cups (12 fl oz/375 ml) milk

1 lb/500 g minced (ground) beef

2 eggs, beaten

4 tablespoons grated parmesan cheese

plain (all-purpose) flour for dusting

1 lb/500 g potatoes, peeled, and cubed

2 bunches silverbeet (Swiss chard) or English spinach,
    boiled for 5 minutes and chopped

salt and freshly ground black pepper to taste

extra grated parmesan cheese to serve

Heat oil in a very large saucepan and braise onion, celery, carrot, and peppercorns for 4 minutes. Add whole chicken and enough water to cover chicken by 1 inch/2.5 cm. Bring to a boil, then reduce heat and allow to simmer for 1¹/₂ hours. Strain, and set aside chicken broth (the chicken itself is not used).

Place bread in a large bowl with milk, beef, eggs, and parmesan. Mix well, and form into balls the size of marbles. Dust with flour, and set aside.

Pour broth into a large saucepan. Add potatoes, meat balls, silverbeet, salt and pepper and boil for 10 minutes.

Serve in bowls, sprinkled with extra parmesan.

∾

Farfalle con le Mandorle

BUTTERFLY PASTA WITH ALMOND SAUCE

9 oz/280 g farfalle (see glossary)

2 oz/60 g almonds, blanched and peeled

2¹/₂ tablespoons butter

4 fl oz/125 ml tablespoons milk

8 tablespoons mascarpone (see glossary)

3 tablespoons meat stock (commercial, or see recipe
    on page 12)

salt to taste

2 tablespoons grated parmesan cheese

Boil farfalle, about 7 minutes. Drain.

Grind almonds to a coarse powder.

Melt butter in a frying pan over medium heat. Add almonds, stir, and add milk. Cook for 1 minute. Add mascarpone, stirring occasionally until melted. Add stock and salt, and cook for 5 minutes. Add pasta and toss. Serve sprinkled with parmesan cheese.

∾

Involtini di Spinaci

VEAL ROLLS WITH SPINACH

1¹/₄ lb/625 g veal fillet, sliced into twelve ¹/₂ inch/1 cm
    thick slices

3 tablespoons butter

3 bunches English spinach, boiled for 5 minutes
    and finely chopped

10 tablespoons grated parmesan cheese

¹/₄ teaspoon ground or grated fresh nutmeg

3 cups (24 fl oz/750 ml) meat stock (commercial,
    or see recipe on page 12)

4 tablespoons olive oil

1¹/₂ cloves garlic, sliced

12 plum (egg) tomatoes, chopped

salt and freshly ground black pepper to taste

4 tablespoons chopped parsley

Preheat oven to 400°F (200°C/Gas 6).

Pound veal slices so they are thin and flat.

Melt butter in frying pan and add spinach, 4 table-spoons parmesan cheese, and nutmeg. Stir well, and cook over medium heat for 3 minutes.

Sprinkle veal slices with remaining parmesan cheese. Place 1 tablespoon spinach mixture in the middle of each, roll, and secure with a toothpick.

Place veal rolls in an oven-proof dish with meat stock. Bake for 5 minutes, turn, and then cook for a further 5 minutes.

Place the oil and garlic in a large frying pan over medium high heat, and fry until garlic is golden, about 30 seconds. Add tomato, and cook for 5 minutes. Remove veal rolls from stock, add rolls to frying pan and cook for another 4 minutes. If sauce is too thick, thin with a little water. Season.

Place veal rolls on serving plates, pour sauce over them, and sprinkle parsley along their length.

Accompany with mashed potato.

Torta di Mele

APPLE CAKE

6¹/₂ lb/3.25 kg green apples, quartered and cored

butter for greasing

1 lb/500 g sugar (for apples)

2 oz/60 g unsalted pistachio nuts, shelled

³/₄ cup (6 fl oz/180 ml) light (single) cream

2 tablespoons sugar (for cream)

2 teaspoons grated fresh ginger

Preheat oven to 350°F (180°C/Gas 4).

Slice apples very thinly.

Butter base of 12 x 4 inch/28 x 8 cm springform cake pan, and cover with apple slices in a spiral pattern. Sprinkle with ¹/₂ tablespoon sugar. Continue layering apples and sugar until all slices have been used. Finish with sugar on top.

Place cake pan in a baking dish to catch the juice that will leak out while cooking. Bake for 1¹/₂ hours. Remove from oven and cool. Remove cake pan from baking dish, and open springform sides.

Reduce the liquid in baking pan over medium high heat on stove, until it caramelises, about 3–4 minutes. Brush apple cake with this sauce.

Roast pistachio nuts in 350°F (180°C/Gas 4) oven until golden brown, about 5 minutes, then chop. Mix cream with sugar and ginger, and whip lightly. Serve apple cake with cream sprinkled with nuts.

2

Winter Menu Two

SERVES 4

Ribollita

TUSCAN BREAD SOUP

~

Bistecca alla Lombardia

ROAST BEEF WITH PUREED BEETS
AND PUMPKIN GNOCCHI

~

Pere alla Vivaldi

STUFFED PEARS

~

ur opening gambit in this menu is a soup called ribollita, which literally means "reboiled". The Tuscans believe the soup tastes best when it's cooked again after having had time to mature, so in theory you have to start this recipe two days before you want to eat it (one night to let the beans soak and one night for the "maturing"). If you're impatient, you can cut a day off the process and eat it on the day you make it. Typically for its region of origin, this soup makes a feature of beans (plus lots of other vegetables) and it is given a dense and comforting texture by the addition of pureed beans as well as whole ones. Thick bread is essential under the soup and the deepest green olive oil you can find is essential on top. In the hills around Siena last century, this would have been a meal in itself. Try to save some soup for tomorrow (so you can test if it really is better "reboiled"), and then you'll have room for another Tuscan passion—roast beef.

We've named the main course after the northern Italian region of Lombardy because of its accompaniments. Pumpkin gnocchi and pureed beets are almost Swiss in style, befitting cold weather and bracing mountain air. We think the roast beef is best served rare but you can adjust the roasting time to your taste. And don't worry too much about making the gnocchi a perfect shell shape—just have fun pressing and flicking them as best you can. They taste so good your guests will quickly forget any unevenness of shape.

The dessert is named after our favourite composer, Antonio Vivaldi of Venice, because the halves of pears remind us of the cello, an important instrument in his *Four Seasons*. Vivaldi would never have known kiwifruit, which has become fashionable with Italian cooks only in the past 20 years, but we hope he'd have appreciated its contribution to the festive colouring of this healthy creation.

∞

Ribollita

TUSCAN BREAD SOUP

7 oz/220 g cannellini beans (see glossary)

8 cups (2 l) water

4 tablespoons olive oil

1 onion, chopped

1 clove garlic, chopped

2 carrots, chopped

2 potatoes, diced

1/4 white cabbage, shredded

1 cup (8 fl oz/250 ml) dry white wine

1 stalk celery, chopped

3 zucchini (courgettes), chopped

1/4 red cabbage, shredded

about 2 cups (16 fl oz/500 ml) water or meat stock
    (commercial, or see recipe on page 12)

salt to taste

4 thick slices stale bread

extra virgin olive oil

Soak beans overnight in 8 cups water. Drain. Cover with fresh water, bring to a boil, and simmer for 20 minutes. Drain. Puree half the beans.

Place oil, onion, and garlic in a large saucepan, and fry over medium heat for 1 minute. Add carrot, and cook for 5 minutes, stirring occasionally. Add potato, and cook for 5 minutes over low heat, stirring occasionally. Add white cabbage and wine, and cook for 5 minutes. Add celery, zucchini, red cabbage, and 2 cups water/stock. Cover and cook for 20 minutes. Add pureed beans and stir for 1 minute. Remove from heat, and leave overnight.

Add remaining beans and salt. Warm over a medium low heat. If there is not enough liquid, add another cup water/stock or as needed.

Place a bread slice in the bottom of each serving bowl. Pour in hot soup. Drizzle with olive oil.

2

Bistecca alla Lombardia

....

ROAST BEEF WITH PUREED BEETS AND PUMPKIN GNOCCHI

PUREED BEETS:

1 tablespoon butter

3 large beets (beetroots), peeled and sliced

4 cloves

3 cups (24 fl oz/750 ml) dry white wine

1/2 green apple, chopped

1 1/2 tablespoons redcurrant jelly

PUMPKIN GNOCCHI:

6 oz/185 g pumpkin, peeled and chopped into large pieces

about 1 lb/500 g plain (all-purpose) flour

BEEF FILLET:

3 tablespoons olive oil

2 lb/1 kg beef fillet, trimmed of fat

TO SERVE:

1 tablespoon butter, melted

1 teaspoon chopped fresh sage

salt to taste

16 tablespoons reduced meat stock (commercial, or see recipe on page 12), warmed

PUREED BEETS: Melt butter in a saucepan and toss beets and cloves over high heat. Add half of the wine, lower heat, and simmer for 15 minutes. Add more wine if mixture begins to dry out. Add apple and remaining wine, and cook for 10 minutes. Add jelly and cook for 1 minute, stirring. Puree in blender.

PUMPKIN GNOCCHI: Preheat oven to 400°F (200°C/ Gas 6).

Place pumpkin on a rack inside a baking dish. Fill baking dish with water to just below rack. Cover with foil, and bake for 15 minutes. Remove from oven and mash.

Pour flour onto work surface, and make a well in the middle. Place pumpkin in middle, and mix into flour using fingers. Work until dough is elastic, adding more flour if necessary.

Roll dough into a long sausage shape, 1/2 inch/1 cm thick. Cut into 1 inch/2.5 cm lengths. Press with a finger in the middle of each to form a shell shape.

Boil a large saucepan of salted water. Add gnocchi, and when they rise to the surface of the water, scoop them out with a slotted spoon and dip in cold water. Drain. Set aside to cool.

BEEF FILLET: Preheat oven to 350°F (180°C/Gas 4).

Place olive oil and beef in a baking dish. Bake for 10–12 minutes for rare beef, or longer if preferred. Remove and let stand for 2 minutes while warming gnocchi and beet puree.

TO SERVE: Warm beet puree in a saucepan over low heat. Warm pumpkin gnocchi with butter and sage in a frying pan over medium low heat, and season with salt. Place 2 tablespoons beet puree in a line along each plate. Cut beef into 1/2 inch/1 cm thick slices, and fan these across puree. Spoon 4 tablespoons of hot meat stock over each serving of beef. Arrange gnocchi on the side and serve.

Pere alla Vivaldi

STUFFED PEARS

1 kiwifruit, peeled and chopped

8 strawberries, hulled and chopped

6 tablespoons amaretto or other sweet almond liqueur

4 large ripe pears, peeled, halved and cored

8 scoops semifreddo (see recipe on page 13)

Marinate kiwifruit and strawberries in amaretto for 30 minutes.

Make small hollow in the middle of each pear half. Fill hollow with marinated fruit.

Place one pear half on each plate with 2 scoops of semifreddo on the side.

Winter Menu Three

SERVES 4

Arancini

RICE BALLS WITH PEAS AND MOZZARELLA

~

Tonno alla Siciliana

TUNA WITH SWEET CHILLIES

~

Torta di Neve

CHERRY "SOUFFLÉ"

~

A rancini means "little oranges" and there is a Sicilian humour in naming this dish that has nothing to do with fruit, but which consists of golden spheres of rice filled with tasty tidbits. The filling is up to you—we've suggested chicken livers with cheese, onions, and peas, but leave out any one element and you'll still have a hearty appetiser. Like so many Italian starters, it's a way of using up leftovers—in this case, yesterday's risotto—but making it from scratch is no hardship. You can make your rice balls the day before you want to eat them, but then we'd suggest that just before serving you deep fry them for 3 minutes then put them in an oven at 400°F (200°C/Gas 6) for a further 5 minutes to ensure the cheese in the middle is properly melted. Our famous Neapolitan sauce is an essential accompaniment.

Next, another slice of Sicily—tuna with a sauce of chillies (or capsicums if you prefer a milder spicing). We urge you to leave your tuna rare, that is, pink in the middle, so that it doesn't shrink and dry out, and so it retains a flavour strong enough to resist being overwhelmed by the chillies or capsicums. The best accompaniment is a cleansing salad of arugola and radicchio (both leaves at their best in winter) with a few drops of olive oil and even fewer drops of balsamic vinegar.

The dessert may look like a souffle, but it is dense enough to be more accurately considered a cake. It's best to use cherries in heavy syrup from a can or a jar, because they retain their flavour after baking (you won't get fresh ones in winter anyway). We certainly don't suggest you use liqueur cherries, which would be a bit sickly. The name of this dish ("neve" means snow) comes from the finishing touch: covering the dome that sticks out of the dish with a layer of icing sugar, like a mountain top. You can add to the alpine effect by puncturing the surface just before serving and dropping in a scoop of vanilla gelato.

∽

Arancini

·····························

RICE BALLS WITH PEAS AND MOZZARELLA

RISOTTO:

8 tablespoons unsalted butter

1 onion, chopped

9 oz/280 g arborio rice (see glossary)

7 cups (1.75 l) chicken stock (commercial or homemade), warmed over low heat

8 tablespoons grated parmesan cheese

ARANCINI:

4 tablespoons olive oil

4 tablespoons chopped onions

7 oz/200 g chicken livers, trimmed and cubed

salt to taste

2 tablespoons green peas (fresh or unminted frozen)

7 oz/200 g mozzarella cheese, diced

plain (all-purpose) flour

2 egg whites, beaten

2 tablespoons fine dry breadcrumbs

vegetable oil for deep frying

TO SERVE:

8 tablespoons Neopolitan sauce (see recipe on page 12), warmed

4 tablespoons grated parmesan cheese

8 basil leaves for garnish

MAKE A RISOTTO: melt butter in a large frying pan and fry onion until soft, about 3 minutes. Add rice, and stir over low heat for 3-4 minutes. Add one ladle of stock, and stir rice constantly with wooden spoon until liquid is absorbed, about 4 minutes. Keep adding stock slowly and stirring constantly for 20 minutes, until rice absorbs all liquid. Mix in parmesan. Cool for a few hours.

Preheat oven to 400°F (200°C/Gas 6).

Place 2 tablespoons oil and 2 tablespoons onion in a frying pan over medium heat and fry until onion is translucent, about 3 minutes. Add livers, cook for 6 minutes, and season with salt.

Boil peas until tender, about 10 minutes for fresh peas or 6 minutes for frozen.

Place remaining oil and onion in another frying pan over medium heat and fry until onion is translucent. Add peas, and cook for 2 minutes.

To make arancini, place 2 heaped tablespoons of risotto in your hand, and form into half a ball. Place ¹/₂ tablespoon liver mixture, ¹/₂ tablespoon pea mixture, and ¹/₂ tablespoon mozzarella on top, and cover with more risotto. Mold into a ball. Dust ball with flour, roll in egg white, and cover with breadcrumbs. Deep fry in hot vegetable oil until golden and crisp, about 4 minutes. Place in baking dish in oven for 2 minutes.

Spoon 1 tablespoon of hot Neapolitan sauce on each serving plate, place 1 rice ball on top, and spoon another tablespoon of sauce over. Sprinkle with parmesan, and garnish with 2 leaves of basil.

Tonno alla Siciliana

TUNA WITH SWEET CHILLIES

40 small sweet green chillies or 2 green capsicums
    (bell peppers)

2 cups (16 fl oz/500 ml) vegetable oil

1 cup (8 fl oz/250 g) Neapolitan sauce (see recipe
    on page 12), warmed

salt to taste

olive oil

4 pieces tuna, about 9 oz/280 g each

Preheat oven to 350°F (180°C/Gas 4).

If using chillies, remove top stalk but leave whole. If using capsicum, seed and cut into 1¹/₂ inch/3.5 cm squares. Heat vegetable oil in large saucepan and deep fry chillies or capsicum pieces for 3¹/₂ minutes. Drain well.

Add chillies or capsicum to Neapolitan sauce in a small saucepan and warm through over low heat.

In a nonstick, oven-proof frying pan smeared with oil, seal tuna over high heat for a few seconds on both sides. Bake in oven for 3 minutes. Remove from oven and drain off any excess oil. Add Neapolitan sauce with chillies or capsicum to pan and fry on stove over high heat for 1 minute on each side.

Accompany with a salad of arugola and radicchio.

Torta di Neve

CHERRY "SOUFFLÉ"

24 savioardi biscuits or sponge fingers (see glossary)

2 cups (16 fl oz/500 ml) milk, warmed

4 tablespoons strega liqueur or Galliano (see glossary)

10 tablespoons whipped mascarpone
    (see recipe on page 13)

12 preserved pitted cherries with syrup

5 egg whites

pinch salt

4 teaspoons sugar

icing (powdered) sugar for dusting

Preheat oven to 400°C (200°F/Gas 6).

For each "soufflé", dip three biscuits half-way into warmed milk. Lay these in a small soufflé dish (about 5 inches/12 cm in diameter and 2 inches/5 cm deep), and brush tops with liqueur. Top with 1 tablespoon mascarpone, dot with three cherries, and cover with 1/2 teaspoon of cherry syrup. Dip three more biscuits into milk, and layer these in dish topped with 11/2 tablespoons mascarpone and 1 teaspoon syrup.

Repeat for the three other "soufflés".

Beat egg whites with salt until stiff. Spoon mixture on top of soufflés, up to 1 inch/2.5 cm higher than the rim of dish. Sprinkle with sugar. Bake until tops are golden, about 7 minutes. Dust with icing sugar to make "snow".

Winter Menu Four

SERVES 4

Antipasto of Fave con Pancetta & Funghi in Padella & Barbecued Eggplant

BEANS WITH BACON & MUSHROOMS WITH
CHILLI & BARBECUED EGGPLANT

≈

Gnocchi Verdi

SPINACH AND RICOTTA DUMPLINGS

≈

Osso Pieno

VEAL KNUCKLE IN RED WINE

≈

Zabaglione

≈

A nother varied antipasto, with a touch of Tuscany in the beans and of Naples in the eggplant, begins this hearty spread. Then we move to the far north of Italy for some Swiss-style dumplings that are so surprisingly light we are calling them gnocchi. The "verdi" part of their name is not a reference to the composer, for once, but rather to the striking green colouring they get from the spinach. Because their taste is subtle, we've sharpened their dressing with sage leaves.

Osso pieno is a play on the old favourite osso bucco, which literally means "hollow bone". Our bones (veal knuckles) are full ("pieno") and after roasting for 45 minutes they produce sweet soft meat and a glutinous gravy that we've enlivened with orange zest. We suggest serving them with soft polenta, which will steadfastly soak up the sauce. Steamed broccoli is the ideal vegetable accompaniment.

Our dessert is a multi-purpose classic beloved all over Italy and credited with miraculous properties. When a member of the family is a little off-colour, Italian grandmothers rush to whip them up a restorative zabaglione. It's a hangover cure, a treatment for anemia, a stomach-settler, a hot breakfast, a cold supper, an afternoon snack, and the ideal accompaniment to any fruity dessert. Here we're suggesting you focus on zabaglione in its original state. Remember you're using Sicily's great marsala wine—the normal sherry-like version, not the egg marsala liqueur.

∞

Fave con Pancetta

BEANS WITH BACON

7 oz/220 g fresh broad (fava) beans (see glossary)

¹/₂ onion, chopped

3 tablespoons olive oil

1 rasher bacon, chopped

salt to taste

Cover beans with water in a saucepan and boil for 20 minutes over medium heat. Drain.

Place oil and onion in frying pan over medium heat and fry until onion is soft, about 1 minute. Add bacon and stir for 1 minute. Add beans, toss, and cook for 3 minutes. Season with salt. Serve hot or cold.

∾

Funghi in Padella

MUSHROOMS WITH CHILLI

2 small red chillies
3 whole cloves garlic
6 tablespoons olive oil
14 oz/400 g any type of fresh mushrooms, sliced
salt to taste
2 tablespoons chopped fresh parsley

Place chilli, garlic, and oil in a frying pan and fry until garlic is golden, about 1 minute. Add mushrooms, toss, and cook for 6 minutes. Remove garlic cloves. Season with salt, sprinkle with parsley, toss and serve.

Barbecued Eggplant

2 medium eggplants (aubergines)
salt
3 cloves garlic, chopped
3 tablespoons chopped fresh parsley
10 tablespoons extra virgin olive oil

Slice eggplants into 1/2 inch/1 cm thick slices, lay them on a plate, and sprinkle with salt. Cover with another plate, and place a weight on top to press down on eggplant. Leave for 30 minutes, uncover, and discard juice. Dry eggplant with paper towels.

On a barbecue, hotplate, or in a heavy frying pan, cook eggplant for 3 minutes on each side. Lay on plate, and sprinkle with garlic, then parsley. Season with salt. Pour olive oil on top, and marinate for 2 hours before serving.

Gnocchi Verdi

SPINACH AND RICOTTA DUMPLINGS

6 bunches English spinach

14 oz/400 g ricotta cheese

$1/4$ teaspoon nutmeg

1 teaspoon chopped fresh sage

4 tablespoons grated parmesan cheese

8 tablespoons dry fine breadcrumbs

2 eggs

salt to taste

butter

4 tablespoons grated parmesan cheese for sprinkling

Preheat oven to 400°F (200°C/Gas 6).

Boil spinach for 5 minutes, drain, and squeeze dry. Puree, then mix thoroughly with ricotta, nutmeg, sage, parmesan, breadcrumbs, and eggs. Add salt. Form into eight large balls.

Smear four oven-proof ceramic serving dishes with butter. Put two balls in each dish and sprinkle with parmesan. Bake for 10 minutes, then serve.

Osso Pieno

·······································

VEAL KNUCKLE IN RED WINE

5 tablespoons olive oil

2 onions, chopped

8 large or 12 small veal knuckles
   (4 servings of 10 oz/315 g each)

plain (all-purpose) flour for dusting

8 fl oz/250 ml red wine

20 black olives, pitted

1¹/₂ lb/750 g fresh or canned tomatoes, pureed

8 fl oz/250 ml meat stock (commercial,
   or see recipe on page 12)

grated rind of 1 orange

soft polenta (see recipe on page 13)

Preheat oven to 350°F (180°C/Gas 4).

Place oil and onion in baking dish on top of stove over medium high heat, and fry until onion is soft, about 1 minute. Dust veal knuckles with flour, add to dish, and brown for 1 minute on each side. Add wine, and cook till evaporated. Add olives and tomato. Cover with foil, and bake for 45 minutes.

Return to top of stove, and remove foil. Add stock and cook for 5 minutes. Serve with grated orange rind sprinkled on top and soft polenta on the side.

∾

Zabaglione

12 egg yolks
5 fl oz/150g sugar
4 fl oz/125 ml dry marsala wine
4 fl oz/125 ml brandy
8 savioardi biscuits or sponge fingers

Place yolks and sugar in a mixing bowl, and beat at high speed until stiff and white. Scrape mixture into a large heat-proof bowl, and place in a saucepan of boiling water on stove. Whisk vigorously while pouring in marsala and brandy. Continue to whisk for 2–3 minutes. (Be careful egg mixture does not begin to solidify while cooking; remove from heat if it starts to thicken.)

Pour into serving dishes and serve with savioardi or other biscuits (and a couple of strawberries if you like).

Winter Menu Five

SERVES 4

Pappardelle Pasta
with Duck Sauce

❧

Maiale d'Inverno

ROLLED PORK

❧

Fennel and
Radicchio Salad

❧

Tartufo di Cioccolato

INTENSE CHOCOLATE PUDDING

❧

Winter (and this book) must go out with a bang, so we've saved our most lavish pasta to the end. Pappardelle are the widest of the ribbon noodles, chosen because they provide plenty of surface area to which the sticky duck sauce can adhere. You should be able to get duck bones for the stock at any game supplier, who would also be able to sell you the appropriate cut of duck breast. If you have to buy a whole duck, don't worry—just remove the breasts to include them both in the sauce, and boil the rest of the carcass as you would the bones. The stock recipe we've given here makes more than the 2 cups you'll use in the sauce, but the liquid can be frozen and used as a rich alternative to chicken stock.

Our pork main course is a favourite in the northern Italian mountains, and we doubt if you'll be craving any other accompaniment than our refreshing fennel salad. The fennel will cleanse the palate in preparation for our most decadent desert. We've named it after the black truffle, because that's how it looks, and of course each plate needs a scoop of the whitest semifreddo, zabaglione or vanilla gelato to create visual and oral balance. True hedonists may care to sit the slices of chocolate truffle on a pool of pureed raspberries.

A long, warming dinner leads to a well-insulated sleep and sweet dreams of the approaching spring, when the cycle begins anew.

∾

Pappardelle Pasta with Duck Sauce

STOCK:

3 cups (24 fl oz/750 ml) red wine

8 lb/4 kg duck bones

3 carrots, chopped

4 onions, chopped

1 stalk celery, chopped

1/2 bunch parsley, chopped

8 cups (2 l) water

PASTA AND SAUCE:

2 tablespoons olive oil

1 duck breast, deboned

9 oz/280 g pappardelle (see glossary)

salt to taste

24 black olives, pitted and chopped

2 tablespoons chopped parsley

Place all stock ingredients except water in a large pan on high heat, and cook until most of the liquid evaporates. Add water, bring to a boil, and simmer until liquid reduces to a third. Strain and set stock aside.

Preheat oven to 350°F (180°C/Gas 4).

Place oil and duck breast in baking dish, brush duck with a little of the oil, and roast for 5 minutes. Remove from oven, and allow to cool. Remove skin and cut meat into thin slices.

Boil pasta, about 8 minutes. Drain.

Warm 2 cups (16 fl oz/500 ml) stock in a large frying pan. Add pasta and duck slices. Season with salt, and toss. Serve sprinkled with olives and parsley.

∞

Maiale d'Inverno

······································

ROLLED PORK

4 fl oz/125 ml light (single) cream

8 slices stale white bread, broken into pieces

2 oz/60 g parmesan cheese, grated

2 eggs

1 tablespoon chopped parsley

salt to taste

pinch nutmeg

2 oz/60 g sausage meat

12 thin slices pork

5 tablespoons olive oil

1 small onion, finely sliced

plain (all-purpose) flour for coating

4 fl oz/125 ml dry white wine

12 oz/375 g tomatoes, chopped

Preheat oven to 350°F (180°C/Gas 4).

Pour cream over bread in a bowl and leave bread to soak up cream. Squeeze cream from bread, and place bread in a separate bowl with parmesan, eggs, parsley, salt, nutmeg, and sausage meat. Mix together well, and divide into 12 equal portions. Place a portion on top of each slice of pork. Roll pork, and secure with toothpicks.

Place olive oil and onion in large frying pan and fry until onion is soft, about 2 minutes. Dust pork rolls with flour, and add to pan. Brown pork. Add wine and tomato and cook for 1 minute. Transfer to an oven-proof dish, cover, and bake for 30 minutes.

Fennel and Radicchio Salad

1 radicchio (red) lettuce, washed and drained (see glossary)
1 fennel bulb, thinly sliced
2 tablespoons balsamic vinegar (see glossary)
5 tablespoons extra virgin olive oil
salt and freshly ground black pepper to taste

Tear radicchio leaves into strips and place in a salad bowl with fennel. Pour in vinegar and olive oil, and add salt and pepper. Toss and serve.

∾

Tartufo di Cioccolato

···················

INTENSE CHOCOLATE PUDDING

2 oz/60 g unsweetened cooking chocolate

4 fl oz/125 ml light (single) cream

9 oz/280 g unsweetened cocoa

4 tablespoons sugar

4 egg yolks (free-range preferred)

6 tablespoons coffee liqueur (eg Tia Maria)

*9 oz/280 g savoiardi biscuits (see glossary) or
    sponge fingers, chopped*

2 oz/60 g candied fruit (orange peel preferred), chopped

Melt chocolate in a double boiler, and remove from heat.

Mix cream with cocoa and 2 tablespoons sugar. Pour into chocolate and mix (preferably with a whisk).

Beat egg yolks with 2 tablespoons sugar until white and stiff. Fold into chocolate. Add liqueur, savoiardi, and candied fruit, and mix thoroughly. The mixture should be quite stiff; if it is runny, add more savoiardi.

Place sheet of foil, about 16 x 12 inches/40 x 30 cm, on work surface, and spoon mixture onto foil about a third of the way along the sheet. Roll foil to form a sausage shape about 2¹/₂ inches/6 cm in diameter. Freeze for 3 hours.

Unwrap and slice roll into 12 medallions about 1 inch/2.5 cm thick. Serve three slices on each plate with a scoop of semifreddo (see page 13), zabaglione (see page 145), or vanilla gelato.

Index

agnello primavera 36
almonds 90
    almond cake 95
    butterfly pasta with almond sauce
      123
amaretti biscuits 10, 31 40, 51
    poached peaches with amaretti
      biscuits 43
amaretto 10, 43, 95, 131
anchovies 50
    capsicums with anchovy dressing
      48
angel hair pasta 10, 66
    sweet pasta pie 87
    with sage 67
antipasto 46, 90, 140
apples 31
    apple cake 125
apricots, dried 119
arancini 134, 135
arborio rice 10, 16, 19, 117, 135
artichoke 16
    fennel and artichoke salad 17
arugola 10, 28, 29, 34, 55, 73, 98, 118,
    134
    spaghetti with tomatoes and
      arugola 55
asparagus
    roast salmon with asparagus 74
aubergine *see* eggplant

balsamic vinegar 10, 48, 73, 118, 134,
    151
bananas 31, 81, 107
basil 49, 73, 79, 80, 85, 91, 92, 94, 99,
    100, 111, 135
    pesto sauce 16, 17
beans
    beans with bacon 141
    prawns with beans 29
    spicy sausages and beans 112
    Tuscan bread soup (ribollita) 128,
      129
    veal rolls with emmenthal and
      cabbage 42

beef 123
    beef with salsa verde 50
    hot beef carpaccio with polenta
      118
    roast beef with pureed beets and
      pumpkin gnocchi 130
beets (beetroot) 105
    roast beef with pureed beets and
      pumpkin gnocci 130
Bel Paese 10, 119
bell peppers *see* capsicums
bistecca alla lombardia 130
blueberries 63
bocconcini 10, 47
borlotti beans 10, 40
    veal rolls with emmenthal and
      cabbage 42
boysenberries 63
bread
    cheese bread 80
    Tuscan bread soup 129
brie 119
broad beans 10
    beans with bacon 141
broccoli 140
    orecchiette pasta with broccoli 85
broth, chicken 122, 123
bruschetta 40, 41
butterfly pasta with almond sauce 123

cabbage
    pork with red cabbage 30
    Tuscan bread soup 129
    veal rolls with emmenthal and
      cabbage 42
cake
    almond 95
    apple 122, 125
    cherry 69
    fig and mascarpone 75
calamari
    calamari with olive paste 49
    fish soup 68
    seafood lasagna 35
    seafood pasta parcel 111

camembert 119
candied fruit 10, 19, 34, 37, 84, 87, 98,
    101, 110, 119, 152
canditi 10
cannellini beans 10
    prawns with beans 29
    spicy sausages and beans 112
    Tuscan bread soup 129
capelli d'angelo 10, 66
capers 47, 50, 100
capsicums 92
    capsicums with anchovy dressing
      48
    roasting 46, 72
    rolled capsicum with goat's cheese
      73
    tuna with sweet chillies 136
carpaccio 66
    carpaccio salmonato 67
    hot beef carpaccio with polenta
      116, 118
cassata 34
cassata siciliana 37
cauliflower 116
    spicy 92
cedro lemon 10, 87
cheese 116
    cheese bread 80
    cheeses and dried fruits 119
    see also emmenthal; goat's cheese;
      gorgonzola; mozzarella;
      parmesan; ricotta
cherries 54, 81
    cherry cake 69
    cherry "soufflé" 134, 137
    quails with cherries 56
chicken
    chicken legs with porcini
      mushrooms and marsala 106
    chicken soup with meat balls 123
    peppered chicken 78, 81
    rosemary chicken 24
chillies 41, 68, 84, 85, 92, 98, 111, 134,
    136
    mushrooms with chilli 142
    tuna with sweet chillies 136

chocolate 37, 87
    baked pears with chocolate sauce
      113
    intense chocolate pudding 152
Cipriani 66
clams 68
    seafood lasagna 35
    spaghetti with mussels and clams
      41
coppa d'autunno 107
cotolette alla pompeano 30
courgettes see zucchini
crabs, sand (blue swimmer) 68
crème de cassis 10, 37

dates 119
dolce dell'angelo 87
dried fruit
    cheeses and dried fruits 119
duck 148
    pappardelle pasta with duck sauce
      149
dumplings, spinach and ricotta 143

egg tomatoes 10, 29, 55, 68, 79, 91, 92,
    94, 124
    see also tomatoes
eggplant
    barbecued 140, 142
    grilled quails with eggplant puree
      86
    rolled capsicum with goat's cheese
      73
    stuffed 47
eggs, truffled 93
emmenthal
    cheese bread 80
    veal rolls with emmenthal and
      cabbage 42
English spinach 10, 123, 124
    polenta, pumpkin and spinach
      cake 105
    salmon rolls 94
    spinach and ricotta dumplings 143
    veal rolls with spinach 124

fagioli 28
farfalle con le mandorle 123
fava beans see broad beans
fave con pancetta 141

fennel 148
    fennel and artichoke salad 17
    fennel and radicchio salad 151
fettuccine 79
    fettuccine con pomodoro 25
    truffled eggs 93
fichi biondi 61
figs 60, 72
    fig and mascarpone cake 75
    figs with gorgonzola sauce 61
finocchiara 16, 17
fish
    fish soup 68
    perch Puccini 18
    snapper with mint 62
    see also seafood
formaggi e canditi misti 119
frittata 90
    frittata di maccheroni 79
    mushroom 91
frolla napoli 101
fruit
    baked fruit 31
    fresh fruit and parmesan cheese 81
    fruit pastry 101
    fruit "pizza" 63
    fruit sundae 107
frutta gratinata 31
funghi in padella 142

Galliano 11, 137
gamberi con fagioli 29
garlic 9
ginger 125
gnocchi 128
    gnocchi verdi 140, 143
    pumpkin 130
goat's cheese 10, 110
    radicchio salad with bacon and
      goat's cheese 112
    rolled capsicum with goat's cheese
      73
gooseberries 63
gorgonzola 60, 105
    figs with gorgonzola sauce 61

insalata caprese 80
insalata di montagna 112
insalata fantasia 24
involtini 40, 42
involtini di salmone 94

involtini di spinaci 124

kiwifruit 63, 81, 107, 128, 131

lamb 34
    roast lamb with sweet potato puree
      36
lasagna 34
    seafood 35
leeks 84
linguine 10
    linguine in cartoccio 110, 111
    linguine with pesto sauce 17

maiale d'inverno 150
mange-tout see snow peas
mangoes 81
marsala 10, 104, 106, 140, 145
    chicken legs with porcini
      mushrooms and marsala 106
mascarpone 11, 72, 107, 122, 123
    fig and mascarpone cake 75
    whipped 13, 75, 104, 137
meat balls
    chicken soup with meat balls 123
meat stock 8, 12
    butterfly pasta with almond sauce
      123
    calamari with olive paste 49
    grilled quails with eggplant puree
      86
    hot beef carpaccio with polenta
      118
    quails with cherries 56
    roast beef with pureed beets and
      pumpkin gnocchi 130
    roast lamb with sweet potato puree
      36
    roast salmon with asparagus 74
    Tuscan bread soup 129
    veal knuckle in red wine 144
    veal rolls with emmenthal and
      cabbage 42
    veal rolls with spinach 124
melons 81
mignonette lettuce 11, 24, 66, 112
mozzarella
    rice balls with peas and mozzarella
      135
    tomato and mozzarella salad 80

mushrooms 106, 112
    mushroom frittata 91
    mushrooms with chilli 142
    perch Puccini 18
    roast pork and mushroom salad 24
mussels 68
    seafood lasagna 35
    seafood pasta parcels 111
    spaghetti with mussels and clams
        41

Neapolitan sauce 8, 12
    rice balls with peas and mozzarella
        135
    tuna with sweet chillies 136

octopus 68, 98
    octopus casserole 100
olive oil 9, 11
olive paste 28, 30, 46, 49, 74
orange blossom water 11, 19, 84, 87,
    101
orata d'estate 62
orecchiette 11, 84
    orecchiette pasta with broccoli 85
osso pieno 140, 144

pancakes 25
pancetta 11, 42
pane rustico 80
panettone 60
    fruit "pizza" 63
pappardelle 11, 148
    pappardelle pasta with duck sauce
        149
parmesan 17, 30, 67, 78, 79, 81, 91, 93,
    99, 105, 117, 119, 123, 124, 135,
    143, 150
    fresh fruit and parmesan cheese 81
parsley 41, 50, 62, 73, 86, 92, 124, 142,
    149, 150
passionfruit 107
pasta 9, 84
    angel hair pasta with sage 67
    butterfly pasta with almond sauce
        123
    linguine with pesto sauce 17
    orecchiette pasta with broccoli 85
    pappardelle pasta with duck sauce
        149

pasta and egg pie 79
penne with saffron 99
seafood lasagna 35
seafood pasta parcel 111
spaghetti with mussels and clams
    41
spaghetti with tomatoes and
    arugola 55
sweet pasta pie 87
truffled eggs 93
pastry, fruit 101
peaches 40
    poached peaches with amaretti
       biscuits 43
    "temples" with peach puree 57
pears 31, 81
    baked pears with chocolate sauce
       110, 113
    stuffed 131
pecorino 85
penne with saffron 99
peppers see capsicums
perch Puccini 18
pere al cioccolato 113
pere alla Vivaldi 131
pesche nel tempio 54, 57
pesto sauce 16, 17, 73
pie, pasta and egg 79
pine nuts 112
    pesto sauce 17
pistachio nuts 31, 37, 51, 122, 125
plum tomatoes see egg tomatoes
polenta 9, 11, 104, 116, 140, 144
    basic 13
    hot beef carpaccio with polenta
       118
    polenta, pumpkin and spinach
       cake 105
pollo al rosmarino 24
pollo alla diavola 78, 81
pollo alla marsala 106
porcini 11, 104
    chicken legs with porcini
       mushrooms and marsala 106
pork
    pork with red cabbage 30
    roast pork and mushroom salad 24
    rolled pork 150
potatoes 122, 123
prawns 68
    prawns with beans 29
    seafood lasagna 35
    seafood pasta parcel 111

prosciutto 11, 56, 60, 61, 80, 106
provolone 11, 80, 119
prunes
    semifreddo with prunes 51
pumpkin
    polenta, pumpkin and spinach
       cake 105
    pumpkin gnocci 130
    pumpkin risotto 117

quaglie del cardinale 56
quails 84
    grilled quails with eggplant puree
       86
    quails with cherries 56

radicchio 11, 22, 24, 98, 110, 134
    fennel and radicchio salad 151
    radicchio salad with bacon and
       goat's cheese 112
raspberries 63, 148
rhubarb 31
ribollita 128, 129
rice balls with peas and mozzarella
    134, 135
rice cakes 19
ricotta 34, 37, 92, 101
    spinach and ricotta dumplings 143
risotto 116
    pumpkin 116, 117
    rice balls with peas and mozzarella
       135
rock cod 68
rocket see arugola
rollata di peperoni 73
rosemary 30, 36, 99
    rosemary chicken 24
rucola see arugola

saffron 98
    penne with saffron 99
sage 36, 99, 105, 112, 117, 130, 140,
    143
    angel hair pasta with sage 67
salad
    fennel and artichoke salad 17
    fennel and radicchio salad 151
    radicchio salad with bacon and
       goat's cheese 112
    roast pork and mushroom salad 24

tomato and mozzarella salad 80
salmon
    carpaccio salmonato 67
    cooking 72
    roast salmon with asparagus 74
    salmon rolls 94
salsa verde 46, 50
salsicce alla toscana 112
sausages
    spicy sausages and beans 112
savoiardi biscuits 11, 57, 75, 137,
        152
seafood
    calamari with olive paste 49
    carpaccio salmonato 67
    fish soup 68
    octopus casserole 100
    pasta parcel 110, 111
    perch Puccini 18
    prawns with beans 29
    roast salmon with asparagus 74
    salmon rolls 94
    seafood lasagna 35
    snapper with mint 62
    spaghetti with mussels and clams
        41
    tuna with sweet chillies 136
semifreddo 13, 46, 107, 131, 148
    with prunes 51
shrimp see prawns
silver beet 123
snapper with mint 62
snow peas 49, 116

soup
    chicken soup with meat balls 123
    fish soup 68
    Tuscan bread soup 129
    vegetable soup 23
spaghetti tricolore 55
spaghetti with mussels and clams 41
spinach see English spinach
sponge, basic 13, 37
    fruit "pizza" 63
sponge fingers 75, 137, 152
squid see calamari
stock, meat 8, 12
strawberries 31, 63, 107, 131
    strawberry "pasta" 25
strega liqueur 11, 37, 137
sultanas 37, 119
sweet potatoes
    roast lamb with sweet potato puree
        36
Swiss chard see silver beet

tartufo di cioccolato 152
"temples" with peach puree 57
tomatoes 24, 40, 49, 54, 74, 100, 112,
        144, 150
    bruschetta 40, 41
    Neapolitan sauce 12
    spaghetti with tomatoes and
        arugola 55
    tomato and mozzarella salad 80
    see also egg tomatoes

tonno alla siciliana 136
torta di fichi 75
torta di mandorle 95
torta di mele 125
torta di neve 137
torta di polenta 105
torta di riso 19
truffle, chocolate 148
truffled eggs 90, 93
truffled olive oil 90, 93
truffles 90, 116
tuna 72
    tuna with sweet chillies 134, 136

vanilla gelato 148
vanilla powder 11
veal
    veal knuckle in red wine 144
    veal rolls with emmenthal and
        cabbage 42
    veal rolls with spinach 124
vegetable soup 23
vongole see clams

yams 36

zabaglione 11, 140, 145, 148
zucchini
    marinated 79
    stuffed 92
zuppa con polpette 123
zuppa di pasce 68
zuppa di verdure 23

Acknowledgements

Our affection and profound thanks go to Gemma Cunningham, who undertook the task of getting the recipes out of Armando's head and onto paper. Without her energy, patience and good judgement, we'd never have got started.

And at the other end of the production process, our editor Kirsten Tilgals, a model of intellectual rigour, asked the right questions and saved us from numerous embarrassments.

∾

Limoges Australia
Janet Niven Antiques
The Belvedere Gallery
Studio Haus
The Parterre Garden
L.A. Design
Redlemans Fabrics
Cydonia Glass Studio

∾

First published in Canada in 1995 by
Raincoast Book Distribution Ltd.
8680 Cambie Street
Vancouver, B.C. V6P 6M9

Published by Lansdowne Publishing Pty Ltd.
Level 5, 70 George Street, Sydney, NSW 2000, Australia

First published in 1994
© Copyright text 1994: Lansdowne Publishing Pty Ltd.
© Copyright design 1994: Lansdowne Publishing Pty Ltd.

Canadian Cataloguing in Publication Data

Dale, David.
La cucina italiana

Includes index.
ISBN 1-895714-76-1

1. Cookery, Italian. I. Percuoco, Armando. II. Title.
TX723.D34 1995   641.5945   C94-910937-1

Managing Director: Jane Curry
Publishing Manager: Deborah Nixon
Production Manager: Sally Stokes
Project Co-ordinator: Kirsten Tilgals
Food and styling: Mary Harris, assisted by Tracey Port
Photography: Geoff Brown
Designer: Kathie Baxter-Smith
Set in Caslon on Quark Xpress

Printed in Singapore by Kyodo Printing Co (S'pore) Pte Ltd.